BE WE!RD

Succeed in Life and Business
Simply by Being **You**

GREG CAGLE

WITH BILL BLANKSCHAEN

To my wife, Angela, who has contributed richness and depth to my Story. She accepts me with all my weirdness and has never attempted to change me. She has been with me in the best of times and supported me in the worst of times. My Story would be incomplete and joyless without her.

Table of Contents

Chapter 1

One Thing Great People Have in Common

"Be fearless in the pursuit of what sets your soul on fire."
— Jennifer Lee

They called him the *The British Bulldog*—for good reason. Short and squatty, bulldogs are one of a kind. Their wrinkly faces host a perpetually dour expression, but they're tenacious and stubborn. Once they grab hold of something they rarely let go.

So it made sense that the British Bulldog would be the one to stand before Parliament on June 4, 1940 in the face of Nazi aggression and utter these tenacious words:

> We shall go on to the end. We shall fight in France, we shall fight on the seas and oceans, we shall fight with growing confidence and growing strength in the air, we shall defend our island, whatever the cost may be.

> We shall fight on the beaches, we shall fight on the landing grounds, we shall fight in the fields and in the streets, we shall fight in the hills; we shall never surrender!

Those now-famous words stiffened the resolve of a nation gripped by fear and facing imminent invasion. They encouraged the people to "Keep Calm and Carry On." Yet few, if any, people in the world could have delivered that unrelenting message of stubbornness in the face of overwhelming odds like the British Bulldog, Winston Churchill. Ironically, that same stubbornness caused him to be expelled from political circles not too many years earlier. But, in their hour of need, the British people turned to the one they knew would never let go—and he delivered greatness.

Every great leader, every successful executive, every high-performing individual, and every person of influence who made any significant contribution to the human story had one powerful thing in common. It wasn't that they were all creative like Walt Disney or innovative like Steve Jobs. They didn't all have the passion of Martin Luther King, Jr. or the patience of Mother Teresa. They didn't all have the leadership charisma of John Maxwell, the homespun integrity of Zig Ziglar, or the effective habits of Stephen Covey. They didn't all have Churchill's tenacity, Reagan's optimism, or FDR's warm way with words.

Nope. It wasn't any of those things.

No doubt, they were all talented. Talent is important, but not enough. I believe they were all intelligent folks who used their smarts to get things done. And I'm sure they were all driven by a compelling vision of some sort, *but that's not what made them great.*

Surely, their natural talent allowed them to do what others could not. No doubt they were all hard-working people who did what others were unwilling or unable to do. But still, that isn't what made them great. Most of them cultivated effective communication skills, enabling them to share their compelling message. They were deeply passionate for a cause that drove them to persevere and overcome obstacles. But still, that wasn't what made them great.

No doubt about it, all of those characteristics are important in becoming a significant contributor to the human story. But talent, creativity, charisma, passion, or tenacity alone won't do it.

It takes something more, something all great people share: *Authenticity*—what I call, the courage to be *"not normal"*—to *Be Weird.*

Authenticity Matters

Being authentic seems too easy, doesn't it? It's simple say, that's for sure. But it can be incredibly difficult to do. Like putting a ball through a hoop or into a hole, it's pretty straightforward, yet immensely challenging even to the best that ever played.

This is true partly because authenticity, the kind that creates legendary individuals and legendary companies, is extremely rare and often misunderstood. Our corporate business culture—and society in general—"rewards fitting in and being normal." We read *authentic* in well-meaning memos aimed at improving customer experience. We're now hearing the word bandied about at leadership seminars, the next buzzword for business insiders. We even see *authentic* emblazoned on theme park t-shirts and clothing store sweatshirts.

But what does it really mean?

By now, you may be thinking I'm just another guy telling you to be authentic because it will transform your leadership—without telling you how. Think again. No, seriously. Think again. Because you're wrong.

If you think about it, you'll probably agree that some have defined authenticity in ways that leave us with more questions than answers. For example, Simon Mainwaring says, "The keys to brand success are self-definition, transparency, authenticity and accountability." Great. But I'm not sure what that means, and it still sounds pretty complicated.

Simon Sinek, author of *Start with Why*, says, "Authenticity is when you say and do the things you actually believe." That's true as far as it goes, but it doesn't go far enough. The questions then are: Why do you believe what you believe? What shapes what you believe? Could it be that there is something deeper at work here, something that drives your beliefs without your even realizing it?

Even Shawn Corey Carter (better known as rapper Jay Z) tries to define *authenticity*: "I try to make music with emotion and integrity. And authenticity. You can feel when something's authentic, and you can feel when it's not...It's just my emotions."[1] So what we're left with is a feeling, an emotion that's really difficult to nail down. How does this help those of us who want to be great leaders?

> **Great leaders choose to be true to who they are.**

So really, what is *authenticity*? How would you define it? Let's keep it really simple: authenticity is simply being *true* to something. So what is it that something great leaders choose to be true *to*? Actually, great leaders, the truly legendary leaders, aren't true to some *thing*.

Great leaders choose to be true to *who*—who they are. Steve Jobs described them this way:

> Here's to the crazy ones, the misfits, the rebels, the trouble-makers, the round pegs in the square holes...the ones who see things differently—they're not fond of rules. You can quote them, disagree with them, glorify or vilify them, but the only thing you can't do is ignore them, because they change things. They push the human race forward, and while some may see them as the crazy ones, we see genius, because the ones who are crazy enough to think that they can change the world, are the ones who do.

Every great leader, successful executive, high-performing individual, and person of influence who made any significant contribution to the human story did so because they chose to be true to **who they are**.

Who Are You?

By now you may be a little puzzled. So let's talk about it. Think about great leaders you've admired, leaders who made a lasting, positive impact in the world. Did they do it by being like everyone else? Did they follow the crowd? Were they afraid to be different? Do you think they woke up every day and said, "I want to be normal?"

Nope.

Instead, they were the crazy ones who got in touch with who they were and ran with it. They took risks because they weren't afraid of what others thought. They saw things through their unique lens and set out to change the status quo. They somehow used their "one-of-a-kind" personality wiring, their unique life experiences, stayed true to their values and lived out their greatness.

Without exception, the path to greatness required them to do a lot of things all leaders have in common—but in a uniquely brilliant way that was determined by who they were. If they hadn't been authentic, how might history have changed?

Imagine Churchill living with orphans in the slums of Calcutta or Mother Teresa staring down Nazi bombers. What if Steve Jobs had tried his hand at drawing or Walt Disney had moved to Silicon Valley instead of Anaheim? Can we even envision Thomas Edison delivering stump speeches in a stove pipe hat or Abraham Lincoln in a lab coat fiddling with filaments?

How well would that have worked out for any of them—or for us? The truth is the leaders we remember most for their significant contribution to history are the ones who lived in a way that was most true to who they really were.

And that's why it's important for you to know something before you turn one more page in this book. *I'm not here to change you.* Far from it. In fact, the opposite is true.

I'm not here to tell you stories of great leaders and help you develop similar qualities so you can emulate them. I'm not going to give you the 10 reasons for this, or the 7 steps for that, or the 5 laws of—*whatever*. I don't want you to be the next Jack Welch or Steve Jobs. Jack and Steve have already been done. The world has already had its "finest hour" with Churchill. My purpose isn't to give you a set of practices or principles you can use to win friends and influence people—although that *is* what will happen *if* you embrace what it means to be the authentic version of you.

Many leaders start with *why*. The great ones know better.

This journey is about YOU doing YOU! It's about rediscovering and repositioning yourself so that everyone and everything around you benefits from your brilliance. I want you to uncover how you're uniquely wired and lean in to, as Carl Jung put it, "the privilege of a lifetime—becoming who you truly are." I'm here to celebrate you—*if* you have the courage (and it does take courage) to join me and kick *normal* to the curb.

I'm not even here to tell you to find your *why* and let that motivate you to bigger and better things. Let's be candid: many leaders start with *why*. The great ones know better.

Why is important, don't get me wrong. But the best leaders start with who, and embrace everything that makes them not normal.

You could even put it this way: *great leaders choose to be weird.*

Chapter 2

What It Means to Be Weird

Greatness, by definition, is not normal.

He sported a Mohawk hairstyle as his go-to look for years. Shaved on the sides, spiked high on top—he definitely stood out at corporate board meetings.

He's worth nearly three quarters of a billion dollars, yet he lives simply in a 240 square foot Airstream trailer in Las Vegas where he's invested nearly $350 million of his own dollars.

He's the CEO of a company known for incredible customer service. Want to return a product? You have 365 days. His hiring practices are based more on who you are as a person than your education or experience. Company elevators have interactive video screens to encourage employees to talk to their coworkers between floors.

He implemented a system called *holacracy* to eliminate bosses and let each employee be part of a self-led team. Anyone who didn't like the idea was offered a three-month severance buyout. Nearly thirty percent of his workforce walked away.

Who does that? It's weird.

But Tony Hsieh built Zappos, the Las Vegas-based online retailer, into a company Amazon bought for a cool $1.2 billion. Not surprisingly, one of the Zappos corporate values is to *Create fun and a little weirdness.*

People of influence, the great ones who shape the world in significant and lasting ways, don't do things like everyone else. They don't conform to others' expectations. They don't seek the status quo. They choose a unique path—their path.

The great ones aren't like everyone else. They're different. They're unique. They're authentic.

They're NOT normal.

They're weird. *Really* weird.

What Weird Doesn't Mean

Before you run out to get "I'm Weird" tattooed on your forehead, let me explain what I don't mean when I say great leaders are weird.

I don't mean they intentionally try to be odd. They're not trying to stand out from the crowd by changing the way they dress, look, or talk.

They don't wear mandarin orange socks in the office (not that there's anything wrong with that) so the boss will notice them. They don't get a purple Mohawk hairstyle to get noticed, or blow bubbles on their lunch breaks so co-workers label then as "zany."

I'm not talking about being obnoxious for the sake of being obnoxious. Plenty of people today in business and society are trying to stand out and be different by looking and acting in the most bizarre manner imaginable on the outside—as if what we do and say defines who we are, rather than the other way around.

What they really want is to be *authentic*—but they're going about it all wrong.

Being weird is about first connecting to the uniqueness already within you, then living it out in a way that delivers your best to the world—and in a way the world benefits most from you.

But wait—there's more.

Reimagining Weird

Why is it that if I called you *weird*, you'd probably be offended? From an early age, we're conditioned to think *weird* is bad.

As kids, we hurled *weirdo* as an insult. We stumbled over our awkward selves as teens, hoping to be labeled *normal*. We carried that mindset into our career, doing our best to look, talk, and act like everyone else. Now we wonder why it feels as if greatness eludes us.

Stupid is as stupid does, as Forrest Gump's momma put it. In spite of all the historical evidence that great leaders choose to be *not normal*, we kill ourselves trying to fit in.

As an entrepreneur, executive coach, and business culture consultant, I've had the privilege of coming alongside some of the top leaders in the world. I've gotten to know them at their best and at their worst. By being in the trenches with them, I've come to realize the great ones do what everyone else does not. They embrace their weirdness.

As I saw this dynamic playing out again and again, I started probing deeper, hoping to uncover why the best leaders choose to be weird when the rest of the world strives to conform.

I discovered a definition for the word weird that captured my own fascination with how they functioned: to be weird means *to evoke curiosity.*

Evoke curiosity. Hmm....

In other words, to be weird means to live and lead in such a way that other people notice you. They're intrigued by and drawn to you. They're fascinated and influenced by you. And isn't influence what leadership is all about?

I kept digging.

As I continued to explore what it meant to be weird, I stumbled across the origins of the word itself. Apparently, our Old English predecessors spelled it *w-y-r-d* (which is weird all by itself).

Wyrd meant having *the power to shape destiny.* The Old English idea of being weird meant you took an active role in shaping the destiny already unfolding around you. Bottom line: to those who started the word in the first place, *weird* meant you had the power to shape the future.

Some have mistakenly associated *wyrd* with the Greek idea of inevitable or inexorable *fate*. Greek mythology makers, always the life of every party, portrayed fate as three sisters randomly rolling the dice to determine whether someone lived or died.

But that's not *wyrd*. (Odd, yes. *Wyrd*, no. But I digress.)

The Old English idea of being weird meant you took an active role in shaping the destiny already unfolding around you.

Do you remember Shakespeare's *Macbeth*? If you weren't too busy trying to look normal in your high school literature class, you may recall the three "Wyrd Sisters" in that play. They appeared to Macbeth in order to shape the future.

So, weird means **not normal**. Greatness is not normal. Weird means to **evoke curiosity** in others. **Curiosity draws people to you and grows your influence—and leadership is influence.** Weird means to **shape your own destiny**. Leaders shape future reality. When you put it that way, *who wouldn't want to be weird?*

Well, OK. Maybe you don't. If you're fine with being mediocre, then you should close this book right now and go back to whatever *normal* looks like for you.

If *good enough* is good enough, then you should stop reading. Seriously. Just close the book and give it to someone who wants more from life than a participation trophy.

If you're OK with living someone else's dream or cramming

yourself into the box of everyone else's expectations, there isn't much I can do for you.

See ya. Don't let the cover hit ya' on the way out.

But if you're intrigued by the thought, it's OK to be weird—not normal, evoking curiosity, and shaping the future—keep reading.

If you want to maximize your brilliance in a way that positions you for greatness, stick around.

If the dream of doing something great and leaving a lasting legacy resonates somewhere deep within your soul, then join me on this journey.

I dare you.

Well then, if you're still reading, I have just one question for you: *Do you want to be weird?*

Well, do you?

I hope so, my friend. *Because you already are.*

Chapter 3

What Makes You Weird

The more you try to be like everyone else,
the more replaceable you become.

Captain James T. Kirk is one weird dude.

The main character from the *Star Trek* television and movie series is bold, brash, raw—and *authentic*. He's true to who he is no matter who respects or accepts him. He doesn't do it because that's what all the best captains do, or because he wants higher marks on his crew satisfaction survey. He boldly goes where no one has gone before and intentionally challenges the status quo, *because of who he is*. Authenticity is what makes him great.

But there is another character who appears in almost every episode or film. This character makes just as many appearances as Kirk. This character puts in the time and effort. This character shows up for work every day, follows protocol, and looks just like everyone else. In short, this character defines what it means to be *normal*.

As a result, we call this character the expendable crew member. He's the first one to be blasted by aliens. She's the one who gets lost in space when a force field fails. You could swap out one expendable crewman for another and no one would know the difference.

And the same thing is true in your workplace or organization. The more you try to be like everyone else, the more replaceable you become.

That's what is so ironic: our insatiable quest to be normal simply makes us *expendable*.

Our insatiable quest to be normal simply makes us expendable.

Captain Kirk, on the other hand, is anything but expendable. Even if the writers were to kill him off, they'd be forced to resurrect him from the dead. He's that critical to the success of the franchise, *because of who he is*.

His authenticity makes him *intensely invaluable*. And you can be too—if you dare to be you.

It's your choice. You can get serious about filling that hole in the universe that only you can fill. You can do you. Or not. Is it risky? Yes. But not as risky as:

- ➲ Becoming the expendable crew member in your organization.
- ➲ Aiming for—and then achieving—mediocrity.
- ➲ Looking successful on the outside but feeling restless and unfulfilled.
- ➲ Becoming what you think your environment needs—only to discover you don't really like the person you've become.

What if the greatest risk you face is not being thought of as *"weird,"* but looking back at a life unlived, a gift of brilliance left unopened, and wishing you had more time to figure out how best to be you?

Your epic story is being written right now, every day as you lead in your office or organization and live with your family and community. The only question is how *intensely invaluable* your contribution will become.

The pressure to fit in and conform has been there since you were a kid in grade school. It's primarily a way of saying, *you're different.* As we get older, we keep doing it, calling out those who don't look, lead, and live like us—as if being unique were somehow, well, unique.

> You are
> not normal,
> my friend.
> You are weird.

But it isn't. The truth is that there is no one on this planet like you. You are, by definition, *extra*-ordinary. You are the only one on earth with your fingerprint patterns. Each of your ten fingerprints contains over 150 *unique* points of information. As you grow, the pattern of ridges with loops, whorls, and arches stays the same.

No one else has the same retina patterns in their eyes as you. It's completely unique to you. That's why retinal scans are used for security—the hundreds of minute blood vessels form an intricate network that remains stable and unique to you throughout life.

Your DNA is surprisingly quite similar to 99.975 percent of the human population, but unless you are an identical twin, you are the only being in the entire universe with your exact DNA strands. It's that 0.025 percent difference that makes you one-of-a-kind.

Everywhere you look, you see your uniqueness. You are *not* normal, my friend. You are weird. But your weirdness goes beyond your physical makeup, as impressive as that may be.

Your personality, behavioral DNA, and life experiences are unique to you, as well. You came into this world with original qualities so phenomenal that only you can fill the hole designed for you. Then life experiences sculpted you further. Events shaped your story—good and bad alike—in ways that only further accentuated your unique identity. Sometimes it felt great. Other times it felt downright awful. But through it all, you became you—one *weird* and wonderful work of art.

And now, in the years left to you on this planet, you have the *only* opportunity anyone will ever have to steward the brilliance of YOU. So the question is, what are you going to do about it?

Someday someone will talk about your legacy, just as we mentioned the legacies of those great leaders a few pages ago. It may be your spouse, children, grandchildren, neighbors, business successors, authors, or historians. What they say will depend on how well you do *you*, because if you don't do *you*, YOU won't get done. And those that are meant to benefit from you will lose.

We probably haven't met, but I already know there is no one else like you. And you know it too. Deep down, you can feel it. When you read these words, you feel the truth of them in your very soul.

My friend, we need you to do *you*. We all experience distractions that can pull us off- course, but the world needs you to fill that space only you can fill. We need you to fill it, not with what you think others need or want from you, but with YOU—the brilliant piece of weirdness reading this book.

You are already weird. You are NOT normal. Greatness is NOT normal. Do you know what that means? Wait for it…

You don't have to *become* great. You already *are* great.

Permission to Be Great

Throughout my decades in business and as an entrepreneur—I've started and sold five businesses, served as an executive coach to CEOs and C-Suite execs around the world, and counseled a wide range of businesses from Fortune 200 to family enterprises, I have never, ever encountered two people who were exactly alike.

Similar? Yes. The same? No. Every single one of them was uniquely weird.

And so are you. What makes you weird, also makes you great.

So many *out there* are trying to discover the secret to greatness from someone who appears to have arrived. They think it's a magical quality that will enable them to wave a wand and achieve their dreams. And that is a lie.

You began with greatness within. The work of art you are—and are becoming, is unequaled in its qualities. You didn't begin as something inferior that needs to be repackaged into the image of someone else.

That means if you can discover who you are and how best to present YOU to the world—look out! Great things will happen, because your greatness already exists.

Wait! Can we just be candid for minute?

What makes you weird, also makes you great.

As you read those words—*you already are great*—how did it make you feel? Be honest. Did you shake your head in disagreement, chuckle in disbelief, or recoil a bit, as if you'd just touched a thin paper cup full of hot coffee without that handy cardboard sleeve to keep the heat at a safe distance? Maybe you're one of the few that believes it. I hope so.

Did it feel awkward to put "you" and "great" in the same sentence? I hope not. But if so, I'm not surprised.

Shattering the Success Box

The world we live in pounds you with negative messages every day. Marketers constantly remind you of how deficient you are—that's why you "need" their products. Your own life experiences may have conditioned you to think you're inferior, damaged, deficient—anything but great.

The truth is your greatness might be hidden at the moment by all sorts of clutter—others' expectations, stinking thinking, pain in your past, or simply an inaccurate mental picture of YOU.

Instead of living out who you are in all your weird brilliance, you may be trying to cram yourself into what I call "The Success Box." The Success Box is the pressure to fit into someone else's definition of success, a common phenomenon in business and life.

No doubt you've felt it. In fact you may be experiencing it right now in your current role. Organizations don't have to try to put people in boxes. It naturally happens as a byproduct of living out company values and culture.

Unintentional though it may be, unwritten and often unspoken expectations about the "right" kind of leader can create a culture that stifles authenticity. When that happens, the potential for greatness is stifled and begins to die. Left unchecked, organizations with inauthentic cultures wither away over time—without a clear explanation as to why.

How do you know if you're trying to cram into The Success Box?

⊃ Have you ever thought you needed to adapt to a certain style of leadership in order to get promoted? Maybe executives at your company are all high-energy, charismatic leaders, but you're an introvert.

⊃ Have you ever behaved in a way that felt fake, in order to be affirmed by people of influence? It might have happened when you applied for your present role—and now you feel disengaged, stuck being someone you're not.

○ Have you ever felt as if you became what your company needed you to be—and experienced some success—only to sense deep within that what you're doing for the good of the company doesn't align with who you really are?

Truth be told, some boxes we make for ourselves. The pressure to be someone you're not or to meet unrealistic expectations can come from within as well as from without. Without even realizing it, you can convince yourself you must act a certain way or do certain things to achieve your own preconceived notion of success.

The other unfortunate truth is that you may not want to know just how great you are, because, once you know, you'll feel obligated to do something about it.

But what if I told you with absolute certainty that YOU—not the person next to you nor the leader you admire and seek to emulate, but YOU—are uniquely hard-wired to do certain things with a brilliance that leaves the rest of us in awe?

The Big 3

"So who are you?"

The giant caterpillar, Absolem, asked Alice that question after she fell down the rabbit hole and into Wonderland. And I'm hoping you're asking it of yourself right now. I'm hoping you're beginning to recognize what might be possible if you truly figured out *you*. Imagine becoming intensely invaluable!

But how do you do it? How do you figure out who you are so you can live in an authentic way that brings your very best to your organization and the rest of the world?

Like leadership itself—and most things in life—figuring out *you* is both a science and an art. Yes, there is a proven process. No, the art of applying that process is never the same for everyone. But that should come as no surprise, because we're all weird. (See, you're not as offended as you were a few pages ago, are you?)

Think of it as a simple math problem: 2 + 2 = 4. I'm pretty sure we can all agree on that one. We could follow that process every time and get the right answer. But there is more than one way to get that same result.

For example, 3 + 1 also equals 4. As does 1 + 1 + 1 + 1. And if you want to talk about doing things differently, try $\sqrt{16}$. For most of us, our eyes glaze over when we see the square root of 16—but it still gets you to the same result doesn't it?

My point is this: who you are is unique to you, so it's no surprise that how you go about figuring it out can also be unique. Yet each of us will likely need to consider the same core components that shape our identity to get the best results. Our paths to authenticity can be different *and* the same (see, *weird* is everywhere).

What remains the same for all of us is what I call The Big 3. In later chapters, I'll unpack how to dive deeper into each of The Big 3 to figure out who you are and, more importantly, how everything gets magnified when you live out *you* in full 4K color.

However, before we can unleash the secret powers of authenticity for your leadership and company culture, we'll need to develop a greater awareness of The Big 3.

Your DNA

As soon as you hear DNA you're probably thinking of the spirally things that make up your genetic structure. That is DNA, but that's not exactly what I mean. For the purposes of discovering your weirdness and living authentically, your DNA is all the stuff about you that you couldn't change if you tried.

It involves your personality, your strengths and weaknesses, your unique hardwiring, your go-to moves, and the things that come naturally to you. These things make *you* and empower you to be authentic and not try to fit into someone else's success box. I'll help you discover your DNA in Chapter 6.

Your Story

Your story is both similar to and different from your DNA. Like your DNA, you can't do much to change the things that happened to you in the past. Your story is all of the good and bad things, the wise and foolish choices, the reactions to life, and the experiences that have shaped you.

If you want to be comfortable being weird you have to take the time to examine your story. Too many people try to run from their story and then wonder why they're living according to someone else's dream. Your story is a unique part of your weirdness. In Chapter 7, I'll teach you how to mine your story for the defining moments that can empower you to greatness.

Your Value

Your values are your key decision-making filters. Unlike DNA and Story, these have some room to maneuver. You get to choose your values, but you also have to realize that your DNA and your Story help *shape* those values. Your values can't run counter to who you are or how you are wired for long. And how you were raised and the story of your life will shape what values are important to you.

Your values give you a framework with which to view life, and they create a means for your authenticity to touch the world in the most powerful way. They help you be comfortable being who you are. In Chapter 8, I'll walk you through the process of how to discover—or rediscover— your values. I'll also share how to recognize, define, and revisit your values regularly.

You Don't Have to Be a Mystery

When it comes right down to it, the Big 3 aren't that complicated really. Sure, it takes work—and courage—to explore who you are. But I want you to know YOU don't have to be a mystery to you. As Zig Ziglar put it, "You were designed for accomplishment, engineered for success, and endowed with the seeds of greatness." It's who you are.

As you learn how to tap in to that brilliance, you can influence others to follow you with ever-increasing influence. You can foster a dynamic organizational culture that exudes brilliance—and weirdness—and makes a significant contribution to the human story.

> **You're going to fill that hole in the universe that only you can fill.**

How awesome would that be?

Maybe you're thinking, *Sounds great, Greg, but... I'm cynical. I want to believe. I want to dream again. I want to remember why and reconnect with that voice I used to hear so long ago that called me to contribute a verse to humanity's song in a significant way. But, to be honest, it's been a while since I've heard it.*

Stay with me, my friend. Keep turning the pages, because we're about to take a journey together and, yes, it's gonna get weird.

You're about to feel your soul rise up again and celebrate your weirdness.

You're about to leave normal behind and finally start where your Story began—with *who* you are and how you can *maximize your brilliance* in every area of life.

You're going to fill that hole in the universe that only you can fill. Do you want this?

Chapter 4

Your Authentic Advantage

---

*The gravitational pull to be accepted and respected
is greater than the desire to be authentic.*

It's ironic, really.

The gravitational pull to be accepted and respected is greater than the desire to be authentic and live out the real you. It's this pull that keeps you from embracing your weirdness in all of its brilliance. It's ironic because when you try to fit in and be *normal*, you give away your best shot at both acceptance and respect.

Think about it. No one ever said *I really respect you because you're so normal!* No one ever embraced you for being so mediocre they could cry. Yet you know you've done it. You've compromised who you are to get a little applause at the office or the respect of someone whose opinion you thought really mattered.

What were you thinking?

Look, we've all done it. It's not your fault. It started when you were two and the people you cared about most in the world hovered over you and said, *Please do it!* while you sat on the little potty. Then you did it. And they cheered and hugged and told everyone how awesome you were. That praise felt really good. That's when it started, the never-ending quest to figure it out: *Where do I need to poop next to get people to accept and respect me?*

The poop-to-please parade didn't stop at two. Remember in first grade when somebody made fun of you packing peanut butter and jelly for lunch, and you begged your parents not to pack it again? Or the time in middle school when one of the cool kids cracked a joke about how a sweater made you look fat—and you never wore that sweater again? The details might be different, but you get the idea.

Like Mike

In the early 1990s, Gatorade ran a commercial with a catchy jingle and an even catchier tagline—Be Like Mike. Michael Jordan was in the prime of his career then. He had won three NBA championship titles with the Chicago Bulls. His highlight reels were dazzling. The North Carolina high school kid who had failed to make the varsity team had conquered his sport. No one else was "like Mike."

But then on October 6, 1993, Jordan unexpectedly retired from the sport he dominated. The kicker was this—he was going to try his hand at baseball, a game he hadn't played competitively since he was eighteen years old.

But when the basketball great showed up at spring training, he looked like a fish out of water. Bob Herold, hitting coach for the Arizona Scorpions fall league team, described his interaction with Jordan:

> The first time I saw him fielding, he looked like a 5-year-old going for fly balls, catching everything on the run with two hands. I told him, "A big man like you has to catch those on the side, with one hand." And he said, "That's how my dad taught me, catching everything with two hands. That's how you play the game, right?" I thought, *Sure, if you're standing still.* And I'm wondering, *I'm really the first guy to tell this guy how to catch the ball right?*[2]

As a basketball player, Michael Jordan had shattered the record books to that point. He'd been named Rookie of the Year, Defensive Player of the Year, Most Valuable Player, Scoring Champion of the Year, Dunk Champion of the Year, and Athlete of the Year. He had even won two Olympic gold medals. Yet when he tried to play baseball, he finished after a year and half with a stat line of 88 hits in 497 plate appearances. His final batting average was a humble .202. At least Jordan had the courage to admit he was off-track:

> It's been embarrassing, it's been frustrating—it can make you mad. I don't remember the last time I had all those feelings at once. And I've been working too hard at this to make myself look like a fool....For the last nine years, I lived in a situation where I had the world at my feet. Now I'm just another minor leaguer in the clubhouse here trying to make it to the major leagues.[3]

On March 18, 1995 Jordan announced his return to the NBA with a simple two-word press release, "I'm back." He picked up where he left off and led the Chicago Bulls to three more NBA Championships for a legendary and unprecedented total of six. His name became synonymous with basketball greatness. While you have to admire Michael Jordan's willingness to attempt something new, he was clearly not performing in his sweet spot on the baseball diamond. Fortunately, he corrected his course in time.

> Great leaders know who they are and choose to live and lead from that place of authentic weirdness.

Great leaders, the ones who do become legends, don't let themselves get pulled off course by the desire to be accepted and respected. They know who they are and choose to live and lead from that place of authentic weirdness.

One such legend was made on another baseball diamond in the World Series of October 1932. It was the top of the 5th in Game 3 at Wrigley Field. The score was tied. No one believed it when the hitter stared down the pitcher then pointed toward the center field bleachers. No one believed it, because no one had ever done it before.

He was calling his shot. It was weird.

But when he hammered the next pitch deep into those very bleachers, he did what he was born to do—and Babe Ruth became a legend. Ruth had been good before that moment, one of the best. It was, after all, his tenth World Series appearance. He was a hero before that moment, but he became a legend when he embraced his weirdness. He chose to be authentic rather than scan the crowds looking for acceptance or desperately seek to gain the respect by doing what everyone else had always done.

Lou Gehrig, another baseball great, hit a homerun right after Ruth in that game and said: "What do you think of the nerve of that.... Imagine the guy calling his shot and getting away with it."[4] Imagine. When The Great Bambino chose to be weird, then lived out who he was in an authentic way, he went over the top and became a legend.

When Michael Jordan took off his high-tops and laced up his cleats, he became mediocre, just another minor league guy hoping to make it to the bigs. Only when he leaned into what made him great did he achieve legendary status. Likewise, when Babe leaned in to who he was, he won the acceptance, praise, *and* respect of every Yankee fan.

However, he did *not* win the praise and acceptance of every Chicago Cubs fan. No one rushed out to buy Babe Ruth jerseys that night in Chicago. But he did earn their respect—and the respect of fans for generations to come. Even as Cubs players booed him that night— fans even pelted him with vegetables—history tells a different story as Babe Ruth's name became synonymous with baseball greatness.

Why? Because he chose to be *authentic.*

The Choice

Unless we're intentional about it, the gravitational pull to be accepted and respected will naturally be greater than the desire to be authentic. You see each of us tends to be drawn more by the pull of one or the other. You may be lured more by the desire for people to like you based on your behavioral hardwiring. Someone else may be driven more by a desire for respect based on their own life experiences.

Acceptance and respect are some of the most powerful forces known to humanity. We feel the pull—and we compromise. We don't set out to do it; it happens by default. We're inexorably drawn to one or the other—or both. Like opposing magnetic forces, they will tear us apart if we let them, creating all sorts of psychological and physiological stress.

But no successful person is ever liked by everyone. The Cubs fans hated Ruth that October night that he became legendary. He chose to be OK with that. In fact, most successful people are disliked by about half of everybody! Look no farther than US presidential elections for evidence. No matter who wins, the number of people who *don't* vote for the winner is pretty close to the number of people that do. Even in landslide victories, forty percent of voters—tens of millions of people—vote for the *other* candidate. When

If you define success by acceptance, you will always fail.

F.D.R. won a landslide in 1936, 36% of the voting public still said, *No thanks!* Ronald Reagan rolled to victory in 1984, winning 49 of 50 states and he still had 40% of the country tell him to take a hike.

No matter how popular you become, some people simply will never accept you. If you define success by acceptance, you will always fail.

We could say you have to be willing to make trade-offs to be authentic. You can't chase acceptance and be real at the same time. We could say half of the people in the world won't like you or accept you no matter what you do, so choose to be you and let the chips fall where they may. And we wouldn't be too far off.

So many people fake it under the illusion that everyone will accept them. They live inauthentic lives trying to get everyone to like them. Instead, they end up not really liked by anyone, because no one really knows who they are in the first place. News flash—if you keep trying to be accepted without being authentic, you're never going to be truly accepted anyway. Not like you could be. You'll end up with fake fans applauding your fake life and fake career. On the outside, you'll look cool, but you'll know better—*and it will eat you up inside.*

Respect is a natural by product of authenticity.

What about respect? Here's the ironic truth: you don't get it by *trying* to get it. The Great Bambino didn't step to the plate that day obsessed with getting everyone to respect him. He did what came naturally to him. No matter how cheered or booed that day, he called his shot. He stayed true to his Story and his Values. He knew the way to earn the respect is to stop trying to get people to respect you and start living out the authentic *you.*

I'm not saying there's a trick to being respected, some secret sauce you can mix with your personality to create a winning recipe for success. Nor am I saying that you can "work the system" of authenticity to garner respect. It doesn't work that way. Respect is a natural byproduct of authenticity. Live out who you are with authenticity and you will be respected by just about everyone—even if they don't like you.

Steve Jobs was notoriously difficult to work with. When he set his mind on something it was nearly impossible to get him to change it. Early in his career at Apple, a coworker coined the term "Reality Distortion Field" to describe Jobs' ability to convince others to follow his lead no matter how far-fetched it may seem.[5] His authenticity and ability to command respect drove Jobs to turn Apple into the behemoth it is today. (And as we'll see later, his absence makes their future quite fuzzy.)

Nelson Mandela spent twenty-seven years in prison, eighteen of those years confined to a small cell in on Robben Island off the coast of Cape Town, South Africa. Yet when he was released, he refused to return the violence on those who had imprisoned him. Instead, he acted consistently with who he was, no matter how many of his own supporters protested. He became the first black president of South Africa by pushing to end apartheid—and won the respect of the world.

Likewise in today's hyper-partisan atmosphere, it's easy to forget a Republican and Democrat who worked together for the nation, not because they agreed on everything, but because they respected one another. Republican President Ronald Reagan and Democratic House Speaker Thomas "Tip" O'Neill were polar opposites when it came to their political views. But each person's authenticity and commitment to their ideals earned the respect of the other and paved the way for bipartisan cooperation in the best interests of the nation.[6]

Each of these great leaders recognized that he could deliver the greatest value by being weird—not by chasing or demanding respect. Respect came naturally when they lived out who they were authentically.

Is there more to it than that? Yes. Do you really have to choose between being authentic and acceptance or respect? Not exactly. I'll unpack more about how this process works in later chapters, but know this: if you chase respect and acceptance, you'll fail to get both.

In fact, by chasing them, you'll miss one of the most transforming truths: your uniqueness can give a tremendous, blow-away-the-competition advantage in certain situations—and put you at a tremendous do-not-try-this-at-home disadvantage in others.

Your Brilliance Advantage

Great leaders become intensely *invaluable* when they recognize that in certain situations they have a mind-blowing advantage—and they lean into it. At the same time, they recognize that in other situations, who they are puts them at a tremendous disadvantage—and they let others lead.

You've felt this advantage/disadvantage dynamic when you tried to force yourself to perform in a *disadvantaged* situation—and you were just horrible at it. It wasn't the right fit, but you tried to make it work. You tried to sell the world on your pseudo-brilliance, and the world was not impressed. On the other hand, when you were in an *advantaged* situation, you were brilliant with minimal effort and your energy was endless.

Perhaps you let fear stop you from living out who you are. In training sessions where I speak on this topic, I'll often ask people who are hardwired to be harmonious to stand. Typically, about 20%

of the room will stand. I ask them this question: What percent of the time do you have an idea or opinion based on your knowledge of the topic, but you do not share it because the atmosphere of the room is too challenging? I asked this question for a year consistently and recorded the results. It's not a scientific study, I know, but the results were troubling—72%! Almost three-fourths of the time, 20% of these teams do not contribute their knowledge and expertise, because they fear being challenged or shut down by their peers, coworkers, and bosses. These are coworkers, not total strangers, and yet they still choose silence. I ask them, "Do you realize that you are allowing your fear of others' opinions to stifle your brilliance?"

I ask the others in the room, who are wired to be more challenging, "Do you want to miss out on their opinions and knowledge?" Of course not!

It is an authentic organizational culture that encourages people to be who they are. An authentic culture magnifies everyone's strengths and renders his or her weaknesses irrelevant. This is the power of *all of us* versus the power of *one of us*.

When you understand who you are at your core, you'll begin to recognize your advantaged situations. Success is built on performance moments, and legendary is there for the taking if you are courageous enough to capitalize on those performance moments. Babe Ruth was a hero before that day in Chicago, but he became a legend when he seized the moment. Ruth was always authentic, whether you liked him or not. He was brash and even arrogant, often accused of being braggadocious. When once asked how he felt about being paid more than the President of the United States, he replied, "I had a better year." He wasn't afraid to lean in to his authenticity. Yes, he became a legend—and so can you. You can seize those brilliance moments when you understand *who* you are, *why* you do what you do, and *how* you can deliver the greatest value to the world. You were born to be legendary!

Be aware: people who become legends don't do so because they always execute flawlessly or hit it out of the park every time.

Let's bring this closer to where you live and work every day. When I first started coaching Susan, she was failing at sales and miserable in her career. She wasn't hitting her numbers, and her boss wasn't happy. The organization was giving her pre-packaged formulas for success: *Here's what you do and how to do it. You've got to sell this way and build relationships that way.* But none of it worked for her. In fact, that traditional approach put her at a distinct disadvantage.

She wasn't gregarious and outgoing. She didn't have the stereotypical salesperson traits. But she did know what she was talking about. She was wired to dive into the details (DNA). In fact, she knew them better than the team that provided technical support for the product. She came from the world of applying the technology she was selling (Story), so she knew the technical details inside out and backwards. Plus, she really wanted to help customers solve their problems (Values).

Once we identified her distinct advantage, I advised her, "Look, just back up and be you. Go in and show them your product knowledge and speak your tech language. No one will care about your charisma or people skills because they'll see the immense value you offer in terms of product knowledge."

Susan did just that. What she discovered blew her away. Customers were starving for someone who could understand their technical troubles. They loved the products, but struggled to use them effectively. They loved the fact that Susan understood their struggles and knew how to solve them. The result? Phenomenal success. She just blew it out. She began living authentically—she leaned in to her brilliance advantage—and became one of the top salespeople in the company.

Authenticity and Company Cultures

The implications of authenticity go much deeper, both for your personal growth and the health of your organizational culture. Authenticity that begins with leaders and spreads throughout the organization can empower cultural change. When leaders fail the authenticity test, you get burnout, poor employee engagement, and a cultural disconnect no one can ever quite explain. So it was with Sam, CEO and co-founder of Ansarada in Sydney, Australia, and one of the brightest tech minds in the world today.

He and three others formed the company in 2005 and chose the name of the company from the first two letters of the four founders: Andrew, Sam, Rachel, and Daphne. By 2017, it had grown to a $40 million enterprise in the highly competitive and ever-changing technology industry.

When I first started advising Sam, he was starting to spiral down a dark path. A natural-born entrepreneur, his innovative and creative daring had given the company an edge. Sam was like a mad scientist behind the scenes, a true authentic weirdo leaning into his hardwired strengths and creating an idea-a-minute that fueled rapid growth. His natural strengths and talents were exactly what the company needed to get it off the ground. But when he had somewhere around a dozen employees, he began doing things he thought needed to be done, rather than what really made him great. Ever so slowly, he stopped being weird.

As the company grew and Sam became responsible for more of everything, he began to succumb to the pressures of The Success Box. He started conforming to what he thought the company needed him to be—a concrete, competent manager, rather than the abstract, idea-driven genius he is. He did it with the best of intentions, trying to help and be what he felt the organization needed. However, over time he became depressed and less effective. That's right about where we began our journey together. So disillusioned, he was considering walking away from it all, even though by every standard the company was a huge success.

Sam had begun to ping-pong between pulling back and jumping in. Some days he would feel detached and withdrawn. Other days he would feel guilty and throw himself into becoming the person he thought the team needed.

He vacillated between cynicism and euphoria, leaving himself and his leadership team exhausted and depleted. Things began to get cloudy for Sam. What was once obvious wasn't anymore. Where he used to be super confident and instinctive, he now found himself questioning, doubting, and overanalyzing. But he felt the need to put on his "happy face" and pretend that everything was going great—even when he felt fake inside. He made concessions to projects he didn't believe in and then had to feign enthusiasm he didn't feel. Employee engagement, while still high, started to slow.

Sam had the self-awareness to identify the warning signs: "The more I tried to become what I felt the organization needed, the more the environment wasn't very authentic to me; I felt almost like a foreigner in my own company."[7]

It became hard for Sam to function on a daily basis. He lost his enthusiasm and the company's direction no longer aligned with his original vision. He and I agreed it was time to step back and re-evaluate. He took a four-month sabbatical to clear his mind and find clarity. Here's what he discovered about authenticity:

> I think about the prefix D-I-S. Anytime you're not being your authentic self, you're *dis*sing yourself, so you become *dis*couraged, and *dis*heartened, and *dis*passionate, because the word *dis* means to negate something or to go in the opposite direction. Anytime you're not being your authentic self, you're dissing yourself. Anytime you're not being authentic, you become *dis*heartened.[8]

As Sam worked to reacquire his authenticity, he stopped the unhealthy and false self-talk he was abusing himself with on a regular basis. He leaned into his weirdness, embraced it, and chose to be true to who he was. He studied his DNA hardwiring. He got clear on his Story and his Values. And good things followed.

It was as if a muddy, turbulent river suddenly became crystal clear and inviting. The clarity gave him renewed focus and passion for the future of the company. With the distractions gone, Sam became passionate about embracing his weirdness and leveraging his brilliance advantage. He came back to life as the inspiring entrepreneur that helped launch Ansarada in the first place. As a result of his willingness to embrace his brilliance, he gave his tech company what it needed most—an idea-a-minute visionary who could lead a bold reinventing of the brand. His company needed Sam in all his weird brilliance—and he gave it to them.

Now Sam's authenticity has reshaped the company culture. He attracts the same kind of weird, authentic talent that runs through his veins. After all, he attracted me, and I'm one weird dude. His DNA is evident at all levels of the organization. Everyone knows that Sam is free to be Sam—and the company culture is thriving because of it.

As a direct result of getting intentional about who he is, Sam delivered the cutting edge idea driving Ansarada today—the creation of a material information platform that unlocks the value of a company today so they can dramatically improve tomorrow. It's a game changer, and it began with authenticity.

Chapter 5

What Lies Beneath

"If I didn't define myself for myself, I would be crunched into other people's fantasies for me and be eaten alive."
— Audre Lorde

It's been said that we lose our way when we lose our *why*. That's true. But there's more to it. When we have the right perspective, we can see the deeper truths about losing our way. Maybe an example will help make sense of it all.

The film *National Treasure* took us on a fanciful journey on the far-fetched premise that there was a treasure map on the back of the Declaration of Independence. At first, the protagonists use heat and lemon juice to reveal the initial clues. But their adventure comes to an abrupt halt when they realize the clues they discovered can only take them so far.

They remain stuck until they discover special spectacles, glasses supposedly made by none other than Benjamin Franklin. As they flip the multi-colored lenses back and forth, deeper clues surface. Soon they discover the treasure of all treasures—but only find their way when they realize the truth: *There's more to it.*

The same is true for you and any team, organization, or even a family that has lost its way. Let me explain. In my coaching and consulting, I always try to get at what lies beneath the surface—to the question behind the question. When you sense that you've lost your way or feel disconnected from your core passion, the question you should ask is not *why did you lose your way?* The question behind the question is this: *why did you lose your why?*

> The question behind the question is this:
> why did you lose your why?

Something Borrowed, Something You

You can probably think of a few reasons why you might lose your *why*. Perhaps you're tempted to find a short-term solution to a challenging situation that has long-term impact on your Story. Let's face it: sometimes you have to survive until you can do what you really want to do, but not lose yourself in the process. Sometimes those life events are positive things—you get a promotion or experience a major life win and figure, *This must be who I am because I'm succeeding.*

For example, early in my career, I worked in sales and was really good at it. I enjoyed quite a bit of success and was promoted quickly. I could have easily gotten off-track and continued my career in sales with that company. But I was fortunate enough to listen to that voice inside that reminded me I was a renegade and would never be happy in a corporate structured world.

Steven Pressfield calls this urge to settle for partial success a "shadow calling,"[9] when enough of your natural gifting gets approved for you to feel comfortable—without fully unpacking all you are wired to be and do. But over time, success in one area can require you to give up the rest of yourself and all you dream of becoming. So you wake up one day and feel completely unhappy and unfulfilled, even though you are still quite good at that one part of you. For example, I'm still a pretty good salesperson, but now that gift is contributing to a fuller expression of who I am.

Here are a few more obvious reasons you might lose your *why*:

- **Circumstances distract you.** You set out in life with the clearest focus and best-laid plans—and stuff happens. Unexpected bills to pay, corporate mergers to manage, shiny opportunities to chase, a million different things might cause you to take your eye off the prize. Tragedy can debilitate you, like an unexpected diagnosis, a hurricane levels the house you call home, or the market collapses leaving your company on life support. Or worse, you lose someone you love, and it leaves a hole in your heart that consumes all your energy for a season.

- **Disappointment deflates you.** You thought for sure that promotion was yours. All the long hours you invested were about to pay off when you got the news—the competition beat you. And you feel as if life just sucker-punched you. When that happens, it can be easy to turn your frustration inward and belittle the power of you.

- **Well-intentioned advice derails you.** I'm a huge fan of getting counsel when making decisions. No doubt about it. But it can be especially challenging to hold onto your *why* when those you love and respect are encouraging you to let it go. Family, friends, or mentors often have the best of intentions, but they bring their own baggage and life experiences that shape their counsel. And let's not forget, that gravitational pull to be accepted and respected only increases when interacting with those who are closest to us. If you're not careful, you can choose a life or career path based on what they think, rather than what you know to be true within.

All these reasons are real, but they are also temporary. We all experience disappointments, setbacks, and distractions. Tragedy befalls all of us at one time or another. I'm not trying to minimize the reality of them, but they will only push you off-course if you allow them to become your permanent reality.

However, after working with leaders from a wide variety of industries, across all age ranges and walks of life, and from every rung of the success ladder, I've come to recognize a deeper, more lasting reason so many of us lose our *why*.

I should warn you, it's not an easy reality to face. Hence the reason we tend to ignore that feeling of disconnect within our souls, acknowledging it means we must do something about it. To confront it means we must come face-to-face with uncomfortable truths about our life choices. But hey, no one ever said being great would be easy.

If you're going to become legendary, with all your unique brilliance you bring to this planet, you'll need to confront this inconvenient truth. Are you ready for it? Here it is:

The core reason so many of us lose our *why*—and thus our way in life—is that our *why* was never *our why* in the first place. We adopted it from people we respected or admired. It was forced upon us by well-intentioned parents who told us we needed to get a safe, secure job to pay the bills. We let other kids in school embarrass us into walking away from who we felt we were meant to be. We let it be selected for us by life events that pushed us in a direction that sort of felt right at the time, but left us feeling as if something was off. In some cases, we choose to conform for the short term, but the short term turns into long term.

We may even experience some level of success, so we figure we must be on the right track—and we stay the course. We keep trying to cram into The Success Box, doing what initially got us the acceptance or respect we craved. But we never intentionally choose our *why* *because of who we are.*

I experienced this with my youngest son when he was in elementary school. He had always done well, and I was told throughout his early school years he was gifted and full of potential. One teacher mentioned he was a natural leader among his peers. Because of his early success in school, he was placed with a teacher whose reputation was one of helping kids reach their full potential.

Imagine my surprise when I was asked to come to the school to discuss his behavior and classwork. According to his teacher, he was being deliberately disobedient and his grades were slipping. Needless to say, I was quite concerned. We never tolerated deliberate disobedience from our kids.

I went to the school ready to "fix" the problem. I asked the teacher to give me an example of his disobedience so I could better understand his behavior. She told me that when all the kids line up for lunch each day, the second in line is responsible for holding the door. Once everyone else leaves, that person falls in behind everyone else as they continue to lunch. When it's his turn to hold the door, she said, he refuses to do so.

That didn't sound like him, so I asked, "Does he tell you 'No, I won't hold the door?'"

"No," she replied, "but when I look back, another child is holding the door instead."

I told her I would get to the bottom of his behavior. That afternoon when he came home from school, I asked him if the report was true. He didn't even hesitate: "Yes, it's true."

"Why," I asked, "won't you hold the door when it's your turn?"

"Daddy," he shared with all the authenticity of a child, "I hate holding the door. All the other kids love being the door holder, so I let them do it."

Wow. He had found people who loved doing something he hated to do and partnered with them. I realized then that he wasn't being defiant—he was simply doing what came natural to him and empowering other people to do what they love to do.

When I followed up with his teacher, I shared my son's perspective and suggested to her that his behavior wasn't deliberately disobedient. But I couldn't quite leave it there. So I asked her a question: "What do you see as your primary purpose in working with these kids?"

She didn't hesitate. "My objective is to work with these kids in a way that helps them live up to their full potential."

Well, by now you know me well enough to understand I just had to dig deeper. I didn't want to be known as "that" parent, but I couldn't help but ask the question behind the question—it's how I'm wired: "Where does being a door holder fit into that?"

After our discussion, the teacher decided to assign him as the permanent class hall monitor to take advantage of his natural leadership abilities. As a result, the teacher later bragged of having the most organized and orderly class in the hallways. The "door holders" got to hold the door, and my son "the hall monitor" got to do what fit for him.

> When you discover who you are— and truly live it out— your *why* will punch you in the face.

My point is this: for our entire lives, well-intentioned people have been trying to make "door holders" out of all of us. But not all of us are wired to be door holders. In fact, I would argue that few of us are. And therein lies the heart of the problem.

We allow our why to be chosen for us, then we wonder why we lose our way. When you realize you've lost your way, you must keep asking why until you reach the only answer that matters: *because of who I am.*

Instead of asking, *How can I find my why,* a better question is this: How can I connect with who I am and live it out in an authentic way? When you discover who you are—and truly live it out—your *why* will punch you in the face.

"Who" Determines Why

What is it that determines your *why?* It's who you are in all your uniquely weird brilliance. Start anywhere else and you may find a *why*, but it won't be authentic to you. Don't believe me? Consider a few examples of legacy leaders and organizations.

Regardless of your faith tradition, there's no doubt that Jesus of Nazareth had a clear sense of who he was *and* that *who* he was drove his *why*. Of all the people who've ever walked the earth, Jesus most clearly started with *who*. He had that awareness even as a young child and never lost sight of it.

He often reminded everyone of his *who*, in spite of the fact that it got him neither acceptance nor respect from the elite of his day. When those in power questioned his identity, he responded simply, *I AM*. It was his firm grasp of who he was, in spite of the resulting opposition he faced, that enabled him to make such an unprecedented impact on the world for millennia.

The same is true of others in more recent history. Nelson Mandela took down apartheid in South Africa because he refused to act in a manner that was inconsistent with who he was. After suffering injustice in a South African prison for more than thirty years, he refused to seek revenge when given power. Why? His values didn't allow it.

When Martin Luther King, Jr. chose to stand for racial equality, and to do so by non-violent protests, it was because of who he was. When Mother Teresa invested a lifetime in the slums of Calcutta, she did so in such an authentic way that there was no daylight between her *who* and her *why*. At one point, she was voted "Most Admired Person of the Century." And as a result, everyone who ever encountered her was inspired to pursue the same authenticity.

We see the same pattern in the business world. At the outset, maverick CEO Herb Kelleher was clear on why Southwest Airlines existed: "I can teach you the secret to running this airline in thirty seconds. This is it: Southwest is the low-fare airline. Not *a* low-fare airline. We are *THE* low-fare airline. Once you understand that fact, you can make any decision about this company's future as well as I can."

Kelleher's clarity on the purpose or *why* of Southwest airlines flowed naturally from his own maverick style. Kelleher told this story to make his point:

> Tracy from marketing comes into your office. She says her surveys indicate that the passengers might enjoy a light entrée on the Houston to Las Vegas flight. All we offer is peanuts and she thinks a nice chicken caesar salad would be popular. What do you say? You say, "Tracy, will adding that chicken caesar salad make us *THE* low-fare airline from Houston to Las Vegas? Because if it doesn't help us become the unchallenged low-fare airline, we're not serving any damn chicken salad."[10]

Harsh? Maybe. Weird? Definitely. But Herb Kelleher was true to who he was, and that clarity gave the entire company confidence in its *why*. Even though Kelleher stepped down as CEO in 2007, the company hasn't lost its way, like so many do when founders leave. Other leaders stepped up who authentically shared Herb's core commitment and continued to move the company forward. As a result, they've recorded 44 straight years of positive net income at the time of this writing, something no other major airline can boast.

And what about Apple? The odd pairing of Steve Jobs and Steve Wozniak as the creative duo behind Apple. In fact, Apple is often cited as a prime example of the legendary success an organization can experience when it intentionally finds its *why* and then aligns *how* it operates and *what* it does with that core purpose.

But that isn't what happened at Apple. Now, I wasn't there with Jobs and Wozniak when Apple began. But I'm pretty sure this is true:

they didn't start with *why*.

The two legendary Steves didn't schedule a meeting to discuss what their *why* should be. If they did, they left out that critical part of the story in all the versions I've heard. Did they select their why, or did their why choose them as a natural result of who they were?

Jobs was a rebel, a "crazy one," a misfit, an innovative, go-your-own-way, rage-against-the-machine kind of guy—that's WHO he was. Wozniak was an inventive, computing geek who lived and breathed technology and was driven by a passion for transforming the personal computing industry. That's who he was.

Does anyone honestly think the two of them sat down and chose to be anything other than what Apple became? Could they have chosen a different *why*? I suppose they could have. A lot of people do. But their *why* would not have been authentic and could never have sustained the success Apple has enjoyed. Instead, they let who they were—their DNA, Story, and Values—determine their *why*. They embraced it, and Apple was born.

Their commitment to starting with *who* is what positioned the Apple brand for greatness. They didn't go looking for their why. They didn't even seem to discuss it much. It happened naturally, because they both knew who they were and intentionally lived out their weird brilliance in a way that permitted each of them to contribute his best. Friction-free? Nope. Authentic? You bet.

After Wozniak left, Apple became an even clearer extension of Steve Jobs. And what happened when Jobs left Apple? Apple lost its way because it lost its *why*—or so the story goes. I agree that Apple's *why* got fuzzy when Jobs got the boot. But that's because Apple didn't start with *why*. It started with *who*. Once *who* was gone, the company struggled to find clarity.

When Jobs returned to lead the company once again in 1997, it only took him eight weeks to recenter the organization because, as he put it, Apple had lost touch with WHO it was. When it stripped away all the other stuff it was trying to be, Apple's mission became clear: "Think differently." It wasn't about WHAT they did or even WHY—but WHO it was at its core and the values that fueled its success.

And look at what has happened in the years since the passing of Jobs. Once again, analysts are wondering where Apple is headed. Once again, it is struggling to find its *why*, because finding your *why* isn't something you can simply assign as a to-do. If it could be done that way, everyone would do it. And every organization would be the next Apple. If it is to be authentic, and the only way to become legendary is to be authentic, your *why* must come from who you are.

It Starts with—a Mouse?

We see the same thing when we look at a name everyone knows: Walt Disney. "It all started with a mouse," Walt was fond of saying, but in fact, it started long before when Walt was learning to become his authentic self. As a pioneering creative, he was a dreamer with his head in the clouds and, occasionally, one foot on the ground.

Walt lost the rights to his first successful, animated character, Oswald the Rabbit, because he never filed the right paperwork. Fortunately for the rest of us, Walt didn't let that stop him. He leaned into his creative wiring one day while on a train from Manhattan to California —and out popped Mickey Mouse.

Under Walt's leadership, The Walt Disney Company experienced success after success. At times, it seemed as if Tinkerbell's pixie dust magically turned everything Walt touched to gold. The company had clarity on *why* it existed. It had a distinctive Disney approach to *how* it did everything. Everyone knew *what* Disney did and enjoyed it. That's because when Walt said, "We must never forget one thing, that it all started with a mouse," everyone in the company knew what that meant.

Mickey was an extension of Walt himself. Walt even gave the

beloved character his voice. It flowed from his imagination onto paper and celluloid. For Disney, it all started with *who*.

With Walt at the helm, the company became the employer of choice for animators and creatives of all sorts. Children grew up dreaming of becoming Disney animators or imagineers. Walt excelled at casting an infectious vision of dreams that sprang directly from his Big 3.

His DNA hardwiring, for example, fueled his creative juices in animation and imaginative storytelling. His personal Story inspired the stories he told, and even shaped the design of Main Street in the Magic Kingdom. The values he chose were family-first and people-oriented. In fact, the very idea for the Magic Kingdom came to Walt while watching his daughters play at a neighborhood park. He longed for a place where kids of all ages could play together—and the idea for the most magical place on earth was born.

There was no doubt about it: the Disney *why* was determined by *who* Walt was. But when he died in 1968, The Walt Disney Company began to lose its way. Fortunately, there were plenty of Walt's projects already underway. His brother Roy kept things moving forward as best he could, but he wasn't Walt. And after Roy died in 1971, other caretakers took the reins.

> They preached one sacred mantra: "What would Walt do?" But they had a problem. None of them were Walt.

They preached one sacred mantra: "What would Walt do?"

But they had a problem. None of them were Walt. Despite their best efforts to do what they thought Walt would have done, it didn't work. Instead of an authentic risk-taker who explored new technology and techniques, the company had risk-averse, but well-intentioned guardians writing the brand story.

For example, just a few years after Walt's death, a young man managed to get a meeting with Disney brass about a short film he had made. As a boy, he had dreamed of becoming a Disney animator. But when he was in high school, he realized he couldn't draw.

Undeterred, he leaned into his technology passion and found another way—computer animation. In the late '60s, computer animation wasn't even a thing, really. And only a few computers on the planet were even capable of creating crude images and rendering them for film. But the boy had a dream—to follow in the footsteps of his idol Walt Disney and make a full-length, feature film using computer animation.

His first attempt was, by today's standard, crude. He invested countless hours in the project, simply animating his left hand in the hopes of attracting Disney support and investment. But when he showed the technology to the caretakers at Disney, not only were they not interested, they offered the young man a job doing something else entirely.

Now don't miss the significance of this: A company founded by the man who pushed the innovation envelope in animation technology failed to see the future of animation, even when an animated hand was moving right in front of their faces.

Disconnected from its *who*, the company slowly began to lose momentum. It wasn't until the later 70s and early 80s that it became obvious the brand had run aground. They were still trying to work with the dreams Walt left behind, but the man who dreamed those dreams was gone. Their best talent began to drift away to other places. Their animated films lacked Walt's storytelling genius and creative magic.

In short, the company had finally run out of Walt by then. It had lost its *who*. As a result, it lost its *why*—and it lost its way.

And the young man whose animated hand failed to inspire Disney decision makers? They offered him a job as an Imagineer, designing a new attraction for Walt Disney World called Space Mountain.

Here was a guy who grew up dreaming of working for Disney.

You might think he would be elated. You might think he would jump at the offer, do his best to squeeze into The Success Box at Disney, and hope his dream of making full-length animated feature films would materialize someday.

That's what most people would do. But this young man knew who he was. He realized he had an opportunity to make a unique contribution to the world through his skills in computer animation. There was a hole in the universe that only he could fill. So, when Disney offered him a job most people would kill to get, he turned them down.

Even though he was unemployed at the time and had no idea how his dream was going to become a reality, he said no thanks to the biggest name in animation. He refused to settle for "close enough."[11]

In an ironic twist, he did what Walt would have done. He stayed true to his authentic self and kept moving forward. He embraced the *why* that naturally flowed from *who* he was. He walked away from the remnants of Walt's dream to pursue a dream of his own.

And, in doing so, Ed Catmull planted the seeds of a company that would one day set the new standard for animation excellence—Pixar.

Chapter 6

Your DNA

No one else is you— and that is your superpower.

Do you recall the fable about the scorpion and the frog?

A scorpion and a frog meet on the bank of a stream and the scorpion asks the frog to carry him across on its back. The frog asks, "How do I know you won't sting me?"

The scorpion says, "Because if I do, I will die too." The frog is satisfied, and they set out.

But in midstream, the scorpion stings the frog. The frog feels the onset of paralysis and starts to sink, knowing they both will drown, but has just enough time to gasp, "Why?"

The scorpion replies, "It's in my nature."

Ask people if an individual can change, and you will get a variety of answers. Some will say anyone can change; others will say nobody can change their *true* selves. I agree with the latter.

In this parable, the scorpion was at a disadvantage because he wasn't hardwired to swim. But he was wise and teamed up with the frog who had built-in advantages for the situation. But the scorpion couldn't escape his nature—his hardwiring—and it led to his own demise.

Now don't miss this: The scorpion was sincere in his dealings with the frog. He fully intended to ride across the stream and safely reach the other side. But the scorpion lacked the self-awareness he needed, so he died *because he couldn't change his nature.*

How many times have you promised yourself to act differently in a certain situation—and you meant it— but when you were in that situation again, you acted in exactly the same way? You kicked yourself, wondering, *Why did I do that? What was I thinking?*

Like the scorpion who didn't want to drown, but couldn't help but sting, each of us is naturally hardwired with default settings that trigger our behaviors, for better or for worse, often without thinking.

Hardwired for Greatness

The power of YOU comes from the unique combination of the Big 3, your natural hardwiring (DNA), your life experiences (Story), and your decision-making filters (Values). But the journey to discover the brilliance within you begins with your natural DNA.

There is a common misconception that you can change your hardwiring. It's true that you can learn behaviors to better apply who you are at the core. Learned behaviors are important, but they don't change you. It's also true that your environment shapes who you are. As we'll discover in the next chapter, your Story shapes who you are; it shapes, but does not fundamentally alter your hardwiring.

That's why it's so critical to put yourself in positions where you can best present your weirdness to the world. In those situations, your natural DNA is magnified. Rather than obscuring you, those situations bring out your best—in a way the rest of the world can fully appreciate.

That doesn't mean you can't do other things well, but we're not talking about being *good* at something. We're talking about stepping into your greatness, not squeezing yourself into someone else's definition of great. And in this quest to reveal your brilliance, good just isn't good enough.

Imagine an introverted, reserved person who isn't naturally wired for an engaging public environment. They decide they want to change who they are—from an introvert to an extrovert—and become a good public speaker. How great can they be? Can they get to the point of good? Yes. With a lot of hard work, they can get pretty good.

But what we're talking about is discovering *greatness*. No matter how much they prepare, they'll still feel like throwing up in their throat a little before they get up to speak. Standing on that stage won't come naturally to them, because it's not in their DNA. Simply put, it goes against their hardwiring. Even if they look as if they have mastered it on the outside, inwardly they're likely wishing they were doing something else. Meanwhile that "something else" won't get done with the weird brilliance they could have brought to the table.

You can't change your nature. Nor should you try.

And let's not forget, they will never feel deeply fulfilled when doing it. It will always leave them feeling empty, as if they were meant for "more." Happiness will remain a rumor, in spite of the smiling face they paste on every time they take the stage.

The same is true of an extrovert trying to squeeze into the introvert box. Suppose someone is naturally outgoing and hardwired to work with people. Engaging with people energizes this person, yet his parents told him he should be an accountant. Imagine trying to become a person who works independently with numbers all day and little social collaboration in an environment that is not all that engaging. They'll go insane. They'll burn out, even if they manage to achieve acclaim and kudos as an accountant. And no one will know why. After all, on the outside, they seem successful. But inside... ah, we all know how that feels don't we?

Just like the scorpion, you can't change your nature. Nor should you try. It's who you are and how you are made. To be sure, you can grow and improve in any area, but knowing and understanding your DNA is the first step to discovering your brilliance.

Where Weirdness Is Born

This hardwiring is where your weirdness is born; it's your nature and is the foundation for building the absolute best you. It includes what some would call *personality,* but it's more precise than that. It covers *strengths* and *weaknesses*, but it goes deeper still. Think of it as the stuff you couldn't change about yourself no matter how hard you tried.

Like your biological DNA, you didn't ask for it, and there's nothing you can do about it. You can fight it, hide it, and pretend it's not there, but it won't change anything. And you shouldn't want to. Your DNA is at the core of your brilliance. It's why you do the things you do.

There is a great line from the main character in the movie *Chariots of Fire:* "I believe God made me for a purpose, but he also made me fast. And when I run I feel His pleasure." What an amazing way to describe your purpose! What might happen if you allowed your true self to follow your natural bent toward greatness? What might the outcome be?

To begin the process, finding the core of your DNA involves asking deep, soul-searching questions:

- ➲ What excites and energizes you?
- ➲ What depresses and drains you?
- ➲ What have you always known to be true about yourself, even as a child?
- ➲ What drove your passions before life happened and crammed

you into a Success Box?

⊃ When do you "feel His pleasure"?

⊃ What seems to give you unlimited energy when you're doing it?

⊃ What are you doing when you feel most alive?

Unfortunately, a lot of people try to conceal or reshape their DNA to fit within someone else's Success Box, because they don't understand their own value. An introvert may see an extroverted, charismatic person succeed, and think they have to act the same way to make a significant contribution—even though they're wired to be introverted, to be a deep thinker and go deep in relationships. They watch as confrontational people are promoted at their company and think they have to be more confrontational—even though they are wired to be phenomenal at resolving conflicts. They see action-oriented peers receiving awards for completing projects and think they have to always be doing… *something*—even though they are one of

What makes you weird and energizes you also makes you intensely invaluable.

the most brilliant abstract thinkers the world has ever known.

You see, you do some things so well, so naturally, that it would be easy for you to undervalue your DNA hardwiring and presume everyone can do what you do. You may even treat what makes you unique like a commodity. But it is not. We all have a tendency to believe that our natural gifting is easily duplicated by others. But that's not true. From an early age, we are conditioned to think that we are not unique. We're pressured to conform, to fit in, to be perceived as being normal, but remember: the pursuit of normal never resulted in greatness for anyone. What makes you weird and energizes you also makes you intensely invaluable.

In fact, the same things that energize you also deplete others. They would happily pay you to do those things for them—if only they knew you had the gift of brilliance in that area. When you try to be someone you are not, you do the rest of the world a great disservice. As Rory Vaden puts it, "Your highest obligation to others is to be your highest self."[12] That's right—being who you really are is the best thing you could ever do for the rest of us. By understanding your DNA hardwiring, you position yourself to add the most value to others and to live your life doing what you were made to do.

The reality is—and some of you may need to brace yourself for this truth—you are wired to do some things so incredibly well that others can't even fathom how you do it. Those things come easily and naturally to you. For example, my father is naturally gifted mechanically. He can look at anything and figure out how it works. We have a saying at our house: "If Poppa can't fix it, it can't be fixed." He is naturally wired with a strong mechanical orientation. I, on the other hand, am always frustrated with my lack of mechanical ability. I place a tremendous value on what my father can do, and he discounts the value of his gifting because it comes so easily to him. If you fail to realize your unique hardwiring, you may think that when people discover how easy it is for you to do what you do, you'll be exposed as a fraud. But just the opposite is true. When you let your brilliance shine, you reveal your hardwired advantage.

> When you let your brilliance shine, you reveal your hard-wired advantage.

Your Go-To Moves

Perhaps the most important truth to understand, and certainly one of the most practical, is that your DNA determines your go-to moves under stress. When the pressure is on, each of us tends to revert to our natural hardwiring. Over time, we may learn behaviors to help us apply or contain our natural tendencies, but under stress, those learned behaviors slip away as we lean in to what comes naturally to us. That's when we get to experience the unfiltered you—for better or worse.

Your go-to impulse can be a good thing when the situation calls for your unique mix of strengths, or a bad thing when you fail to realize you're vulnerable because of your wiring. If the scorpion had been self-aware, he may not have drowned on the back of the frog.

If you fail to discover your DNA and how to manage it well, you'll be tempted to try to be everything to everyone, in every situation—and make yourself expendable instead of invaluable. Worse, you'll frustrate everyone around you who already knows you're struggling—even if you think you're concealing it well.

Understanding how you are wired means you'll know your natural tendencies under stress. You can put safeguards in place. You'll know when to lead and when to team. You'll know when to charge the hill and when to stay with the supplies because the battle calls for someone with different strengths. And you'll learn to not only be OK with that, you'll seek out opportunities to let both your brilliance and the brilliance of others shine. When that level of authenticity occurs, organizational greatness follows.

Think again about those two founders of Apple Computers—Steve Jobs and Steve Wozniak. Remember that one was hardwired to be an abstract innovator. The other was hardwired to be a concrete innovator. Both were innovators, but they went about it in different ways. Had one tried to play the role of the other, I wouldn't be typing these words on an Apple computer. We would never have known the iPod or iPhone. The world would be a very different place.

They created a culture early on at Apple that freed each of them to do what they did best. Authenticity begat authenticity—and greatness was born. Apply this principle to any team or organization you lead and the world *will* notice.

The Science behind Your Weirdness

There are 6 key ways you are wired to be weird. So how do you figure out your hardwiring? It's not as if a doctor slaps an ingredients label on you when you're born. Imagine what the world would be like if each of us could simply scan a barcode to discover and auto-align our strengths. That day may come, but until then it's up to each of us to be intentional about discovering and communicating our natural hardwiring.

In my experience of working in the trenches alongside thousands of high-performing people like yourself, experience that is corroborated by data from the most accurate assessment, there are six key ways to be weird that greatly impact your ability to deliver your best to the world.

These six are not exhaustive, by any means, but they address most of the pain points you feel when interacting with others and help to identify your greatest opportunity to shine. It's important to realize that these six spectrums do not make judgments. They don't reveal what's right or wrong with you (for that you can ask your parents, spouse, or, better yet, your kids). One is not superior to the other. And where your hardwiring falls on each spectrum is neither good nor bad. It simply reflects who you are. What you do with that knowledge, however, is what makes all the difference.

Furthermore, each spectrum can be divided into preferences people have based on a random distribution of results. Roughly ⅓ of us will find ourselves preferring one response while another third prefers the opposite. Meanwhile another ⅓ will be wired to adapt to the situation. In other words, based on the data, our natural hardwiring strengths are evenly distributed amongst us all. Imagine that! None of us have all we need for every situation. We *need* each other.

But that's not all. Everyone's hardwiring varies in intensity.

(Remember, these preferences are neither bad nor good in and of themselves.) So, as we walk through these six ways to be weird, know that you are probably have an adaptive preference for some and far more intense preferences in others.

As you read through this list, be sure to listen to that little voice inside that tries to tells you who you really are. Ready? Here we go:

1. **Control.** Do you prefer to take charge or let someone else lead? Each of us has a natural hardwiring that affects our default responses to situations.

   ● **Accommodating:** You're often viewed as accommodating, relaxed, and supportive. You might shine at building consensus and a team spirit and are often described as being tactful or diplomatic. You're motivated with an underlying desire to fit in and avoid rocking the boat.

   ● **Directive:** You read the description above and wince. You're already shaking your head, just itching to take action. Your default motivation is to take control. You tend to be viewed as direct, frank, or even bold. Situations that call for immediate action are your moments to shine.

   ● **Adaptive:** You could go either way depending on the situation. You could step up and take charge just as easily as let someone else drive. It often depends on other factors in play at that time. You'll often be viewed as flexible or diverse when it comes to being in control.

2. **Interaction.** How do you prefer to interact with other people? Are you a natural introvert or an extrovert? Remember, being an introvert or extrovert has nothing to do with whether or not you like people. It's about how you recharge. Introverts recharge

by withdrawing from interaction with others. Extroverts get recharged by engaging others. So, your preferences here don't determine your ability to interact, but they do reveal your default setting, which you must understand in order to position yourself to deliver your best.

⊃ **Introvert:** You need down time to recharge. If you don't get it, you're in trouble. You tend to be seen as serious, reserved, or quiet at times. You tend to be more task-oriented, a good listener, and work well alone. You're often focused on getting things done instead of hanging out and chatting. You're motivated to avoid attention and reflect.

⊃ **Extrovert:** You're wired to be more extroverted and motivated to gain attention and express yourself to others. You're often seen as enthusiastic, verbal, and social—a people person. You may be viewed as talkative, gregarious, and lighthearted.

⊃ **Adaptive:** You could go either way, depending on the situation. Now, to be sure, everyone falls on one side or the other of the introvert / extrovert spectrum, but those in the middle tend to be able to easily shift between the two worlds because of their hardwiring. And when they aren't able to recharge fully, it doesn't seem to impact them as greatly as those who place on either side of the spectrum. Once again, the key word here in the middle is *flexible.*

3. **Conflict and Pace.** Did you know you are hardwired to respond to conflict and challenges in a certain way? You can and should still choose your response to each situation, but if you don't know your default setting, you'll be at a disadvantage every time.

⊃ **Challenging:** You tend to be more emotionally detached. It's not that you don't care about people, but your instinctive reaction is to challenge, to be action-oriented and logical rather than empathetic and touchy-feely. You're generally more goal- and results-oriented and like fast-paced, quick decisions. Because of your hardwiring, you tend to be seen as eager, objective, thick-skinned, or questioning. You're motivated to effect change and apply logic.

- **Harmonious:** You are way more emotionally engaged. You're often be viewed as being more compassionate, harmonious, and understanding. Your default setting is to be patient, supportive, and sympathetic. You'd rather hug it out than slug it out—or analyze it. You're motivated to ensure stability and show compassion.

- **Adaptive:** You're wired to show both set of traits to some degree depending on the situation. You're not the first to cry, but your eyes won't be dry. You see the value of logic and getting results, but you'll readily offer a hug when needed. You'll engage in change efforts, but also be concerned about how everyone feels about it to some degree.

4. **Order.** Are you the kind of person who likes to wing it or to prepare to the nth degree? Does it bother you when no one else appreciates the value of preparation or when some people (I won't name any names, but… my wife) seem to take forever to get up to speed? There's a reason for both—how people are hardwired to deal with structure, details, and the need to prepare.

- **Spontaneous:** You aren't simply "messy," as those on the right side like to think. You are literally hardwired to be sponta-neous, flexible, versatile, and instinctive. As a result, you can react quickly to challenges and "think on your feet," improvise and work with generalities rather than specifics. You don't want to "get lost in the weeds" and are motivated to pursue greater freedom and flexibility.

○ **Methodical**: You are methodical and always well-prepared. You may be viewed as precise, organized, and achieving. You emphasize getting it right and thrive "in the details." You're often highly scheduled, and "on-time" means arriving early. You are naturally motivated to pursue accuracy and structure.

○ **Adaptive:** You could naturally apply to some degree in either direction depending on the situation. You simply don't have intense inclinations in either direction, although as we'll see later, your Story could shape your tendencies or the values that determine how you apply yourself here.

5. **Adventure.** Why do some people like jumping out of perfectly good airplanes while others would never play rock-paper-scissors for fear of losing? A lot of it has to do with how we're hardwired. We each have a natural response to risk-taking that is at the heart of who we are and how we live that out.

○ **Cautious:** Cautious—that's the word to describe you. Naturally risk-averse, you can be viewed as careful, steady, or consistent. People always know what they're going to get when interacting with you. You can be seen as guarded or balanced and are motivated to minimize risk wherever possible.

○ **Adventurous:** As a pioneer, you're the one who tends to leap, then look. Adventurous, courageous, ambitious—all of those labels might be applied to you. You're often more competitive (You'll not only play rock-paper-scissors, you'll keep playing until you win!). Far from being risk-averse, you like taking risks and exploring new frontiers.

○ **Adaptive:** Yep. You guessed it. It depends. You're wired to do both to some degree depending on the situation. It's not that you don't care, mind you. But you just aren't wired to be as intense in this area. If a friend is already skydiving, you might happily go along. Or if another friend sits out a ride on a roller coaster, you might do the same to keep them company.

6. **Innovation.** Are you an abstract thinker or a concrete thinker? And what difference does it make? Remember earlier when I mentioned how Steve Jobs and Steve Wozniak let each other fully express their authenticity—and a great organization resulted? I said that one of them was a brilliant *abstract* thinker and one was an equally brilliant *concrete* thinker.

But which was which?

I've asked this question in countless training experiences over the years and I am always amazed at how many times I get the same answer. What do *you* think? Was Jobs or Wozniak the abstract innovator?

Usually I get this answer, often without any hesitation: *Well, of course, Steve Jobs was an abstract innovator. I mean look at what he created—the Mac family of personal computers, the iPod, the iPhone.*

But hold on…. If that was your answer, you just named three very concrete items. Those are not ideas on a whiteboard, but products you can hold in your hands. And you're right, Steve Jobs was the wizard who brought those to the market. But it was Steve Wozniak who laid the foundation for abstract innovation at Apple. Wozniak brought the ideas of "what could be" in the computer world. In fact it was Wozniak who had the idea of a personal computer when there was no such thing. Jobs took that abstract innovation and applied his own concrete innovation and voilà—the iRevolution. Jobs was the concrete innovator, Wozniak the abstract innovator.

You might think of the difference between the two in this way: The abstract innovator sees a disheveled pile of papers and imagines how a thin piece of metal might be manipulated to help hold them together—and the paper clip is born.

But a concrete innovator sees papers still slipping out from beneath that paperclip and imagines adding ridges to the metal to solve the problem.

Abstract innovation gives us the digital technology to store thousands of files on a portable device. Concrete innovation gives us "a thousand songs in your pocket."

So are you wired to be more abstract or concrete in your innovation?

- ➲ **Concrete:** You are hanging with Steve Jobs! Concrete, experiential, real-world—that's you. You might even be described as being analytical, but you're always asking, "How can this work better on a practical level?" Consequently, you may be viewed as being better at mechanical tasks or assembling things. You are imaginative and creative, but in a tangible, real-world way.

- ➲ **Abstract:** You're an abstract innovator like Wozniak! You're also imaginative, but in the realm of ideas, thoughts, and intellect. You're often viewed as being highly intelligent, clever, or original for your out-of-the-box thinking. You might connect things in ways no one else sees or discover ways to leverage resources that seem to elude others. You're motivated by a desire to think differently about, well, everything.

- ➲ **Adaptive:** You're able to dip into both the abstract and the concrete and make sense of it all. You may not be naturally wired to display intense traits here, but you can grasp both and use that to your advantage. After all, someone was needed to actually lead Apple once Wozniak and Jobs were done innovating—without losing the essence of both—and in a creative, innovative fashion.

There you have it. The science behind your weird. Now, why does any of this matter?

Why Your Wiring Matters

When you understand how you are naturally hardwired in these 6 key areas, you're empowered to deliver your very best to the world. No longer do you see your weirdness as odd or something to be ashamed of. Just the opposite—your DNA is cause to celebrate. But it's also why you struggle so much sometimes to interact with others.

Not surprisingly, most of our workplace struggles stem from people problems. Just looking at the above list explains a lot of where those struggles come from. Imagine that someone is wired to be methodical and detail-oriented. What's their instinctive reaction when someone who is hard-wired to be spontaneous brings a new idea and tells them all the reasons why it's something they should support—but provides very little detail or structure on how it can be implemented?

The reaction is likely to be: *This is a half-baked idea. It can't be any good. No detail and it hasn't been thought through.* The truth is that it may be the best idea ever, but the detail-oriented person doesn't endorse it, because it lacks the detail they need to get on board. The long-term effect on the relationship between these two people is disconnect. The spontaneous person will eventually disconnect from the methodical person, feeling like they are too rigid and resistant to change. The methodical person will disconnect from the spontaneous person, thinking they are shallow and shoot from the hip too much.

Now the reality is that each person is doing what comes naturally! Neither one of them is right or wrong, but because they don't understand the hardwiring at work, they default to misunderstanding.

In fact, that's the first and most easily-recognizable hazard of not understanding how you're hardwired—a tendency to disconnect from those who are different.

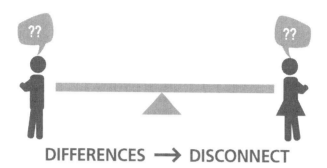

DIFFERENCES ⟶ DISCONNECT

Disconnect can occur whenever two people are wired to place on opposite ends of a given spectrum. Think of the frog and the scorpion. In the situation I described above, the accommodating person doesn't understand the directing person—so they fill in the blanks with their worst fears. But imagine how that meeting might unfold differently if each of them not only understood their own strengths, but were able to freely discuss how to best position themselves to make the highest contribution to the team in that situation? What high-powered performances might result then? Instead of those differences subtracting from productivity, they can be leveraged to multiply it. (That's the power of a weird culture, by the way. More on that later.)

And the frog and scorpion? They just might have made it across the water. For example, imagine if the self-aware scorpion had offered to sit on a protective mat to protect the frog from its sting. Or what if the frog had suggested the scorpion tie its stinger in place? The options to prevent the problem are endless—but they can be considered only once you are aware of the natural hardwiring.

But there is another destructive dynamic that can be even more dangerous because it tends to sneak up on us. Let's face it, we tend to gravitate toward people we most easily understand, don't we? The saying "opposites attract" is true to the extent that sparks usually fly when they collide.

There is another cliché at work in most workplace situations: "Birds of a feather flock together." We like to hang out with people we deem to be like us—in this case, people who are wired in a similar fashion. If we're wired to be accommodating, we'll tend to spend time with others who share those traits. If we're risk takers, we'll prefer to jump out of planes with them, because they "get" us. But over time, similar hardwiring can actually create a lot of problems—not the disconnect caused by opposites, but a sandpaper effect that comes from two people being too similar.

I've often seen this dynamic play out between business partners who got along great when they started the company, but ran into serious friction as the venture grew. Over time, their similarities rubbed one another the wrong way, and the friction produced heat—and a lot of it. Both effects can harm you individually and utterly destroy entire organizations when the disconnect of friction affects leadership.

SIMILARITIES → FRICTION

Imagine if the scorpion had teamed up with another scorpion to cross the water. No doubt they would have gotten along great, totally understanding about the whole "can't help but sting thing." But they would have been in for some serious disappointment when they tried to cross the water. No matter how much one insisted that the other should learn to swim, it wouldn't have happened. Similar? Yes. Successful? No.

> No matter how you are naturally hardwired, you can learn to lead and succeed by leveraging your own unique brilliance.

But it doesn't have to be this way. No matter how you are naturally hardwired, you can learn to lead and succeed by leveraging your own unique brilliance. And here's the truly empowering part: once you become aware of your own weird brilliance, you can empower people around you—on your team, in your organization, or even in your family—to do the same. And that's when the real magic begins.

Bridge-Builders

Most of the examples so far have focused on people who place either to the right or left on the spectrum on the "Ways to Be Weird" list. But that's only ⅔ of the population. What if you think you might be in the middle on some of them (and just about everybody is)? What then? Are you just an afterthought? What special powers do you have, if any?

Good news. You are a bridge-builder. Your natural gifting lies in your ability to easily adapt in those areas. Your adaptability positions you to understand the language others speak on both extremes of that spectrum. Every organization or team needs people who are wired to be in the middle—to bridge the gap between the talent on either side of each spectrum. You are the catalysts that make everything work smoothly in those areas. When you apply your hardwiring intentionally with self-awareness and social awareness, the team really begins to maximize its performance.

When differences produce disconnect, you are the one who

saves the day. Why? Because you understand both sides! You know what it feels like to be accommodating and directing. You get the value of being quiet at times and enjoying time spent engaging people. You grasp the power of logic, but also empathize with those who need a hug. Your desk may not be the neatest all the time, but you understand the value of organization while you toss out some creative ideas. You're the stable one who keeps the risk-takers grounded and pulls the cautious ones from their bunkers.

In short, you are invaluable no matter where you place yourself on each of the spectrums. If you are more intense in one area, you have a special talent to bring what few can. But if you find yourself in the mid-range, you also have a unique opportunity to understand and leverage that understanding to lead and empower others to succeed.

And what if you are in the mid-range on all 6 areas? You are an Adapter (approx. 8% of the population), the glue that holds teams together. You excel at bridging the gap and bringing people together in powerful ways that elude others.

Each of us has a unique hard-wired brilliance that, when properly understood, gives us an opportunity to most fully reveal the greatness within. Understanding your DNA is the first part of the Big 3 and where your quest to discover your brilliance must begin. But it must not end there. There is, quite literally, more to the Story of YOU.

Chapter 7

Your Story

To be who you are, you cannot ignore the experiences that have shaped you.

Few people can boast of having a Story quite so compelling as Louis Zamperini. An excellent long-distance runner who competed in the 1936 Olympic Games in Berlin, Hitler himself met him after the race and said, "Aha! The boy with the fast finish!" When the 1940 Tokyo Olympics were set aside by the war, Zamperini joined the Army Air Corps and trained as a Bombardier.

In 1943 on a search and rescue mission about 800 miles south of Hawaii, his B-24 bomber went down. He was one of only three survivors. They drifted in a rubber life raft for 2,000 miles with little water and no food. They battled the sun, avoiding Japanese aircraft, sharks, and dehydration. After forty-seven days, they arrived on the Marshall Islands—and his situation went from worse to horrific. He was immediately captured by the Japanese army and sent to a prisoner of war camp. For the next two and a half years, he would face torture, forced medical experiments, beatings, and starvation at the hands of sadistic guards. His captors took perverse pleasure in making him suffer, while back home his parents were told he was dead.

After the war, Louis was filled with bitterness and anger towards his captors. He often dreamed of killing them. One night, he awoke from a nightmare with his hands around his wife's neck, choking her. He eventually turned to alcohol to escape the pain. Louis' Story could have stopped there. He could have been one more walking war casualty, broken and wounded. But when his wife threatened to leave him, he knew he had to change the direction of his Story.

She invited him to hear a young preacher named Billy Graham, something Louis was reluctant to do. It was then that Graham's message of forgiveness resonated within his heart, and his Story was forever changed.

As Zamperini described it, "I momentarily flashed to the life raft in the Pacific, the moment when I prayed to God that if He spared my life, that I'd dedicate it to service and prayer – you know all those promises you make when you're in a jam. I realized then that I'd turned my back on my promises and on God. And when I got off my knees that day in the tent, I knew I would be through with drinking, smoking and revenge fantasies."[13]

From that point on, Zamperini sought out his captors and forgave them one by one. He spent the rest of his long life touring and speaking a message of forgiveness and reconciliation, His Story is compelling and powerful, a mix of circumstance and choice, just like you and your Story.

You don't have to be an Olympic athlete, survivor of a plane crash, adrift at sea, prisoner of war, and hero to have a powerful Story. It turns out your Story is compelling too, because it is your Story—unique and powerful. And when you understand how your Story shapes you, you can embrace this second key component of figuring out who you are and maximizing that brilliance.

Your Story Contributes to Your Identity

If your DNA hardwiring is how you are made, then your Story is how your life has unfolded, including the choices you've made and what you've learned from them.

Your life's Story adds an additional dimension to your identity. Like your DNA, the events and twists and turns of your life are unique to you. No one else on the planet has had the exact same life experiences as you. You've experienced losses, pain, success, failure, joy, and sadness, along with life-defining moments. Your life's Story is *as important* to who you are as your DNA hardwiring.

Your Story is your life. Some things have happened to you. Some things you've made happen. You've made good choices and bad choices. You've fallen in love. You've fallen out of love. You have moments of intense happiness and deep regret. You were crushed by an economic collapse. You married your high school sweetheart. You climbed to the top of Mount Kilimanjaro. You went fishing with your grandfather. Whatever the events have been for you, it's your Story—and it has shaped who you are.

How have these experiences shaped you? Do you know your own Story? Many of us live what Aristotle called the "unexamined life." I'm amazed at how many times I've asked people to share some of their defining moments in life—and they can't tell me. Yet after they think about it, they have several. They simply hadn't thought about it before. What are yours?

Few of us ever take the time to reflect on our stories. Life is something that just sort of happens *to* us, and we roll with it without much intentional thought. Instead of choosing to respond, we re-act, and end up making career and life choices without ever realizing how our life experiences have pushed us into a box. As long as we live an unexamined life, greatness will elude us.

> As long as we live an unexamined life, greatness will elude us.

Instead of ignoring your Story, what if you intentionally remembered your defining moments when you changed your direction, your thought process, or your view of the world? Those changes usually happen as a result of:

- Family Influences
- Victory and Defeat
- Celebration and Loss
- Acceptance and Rejection
- Choices and Consequences
- Pleasure and Pain

When you take the time to figure out what changed in your Story and why, you free yourself to unleash your brilliance to the world, unhindered by unintentional baggage. In doing so, you position yourself for greatness.

Negative Programming

Like your DNA hardwiring, you can't change a lot of what has happened to you. You didn't choose your parents, where you lived as a child, or most of the things that happened to you, positive and negative. These negative experiences often trigger emotional responses within us that then fuel our actions—even though we may not realize why. For example, we feel our stomach churn when the boss sends an email without realizing that we're reacting to some overbearing authority figure in our lives from decades ago. When our defenses go up in a conversation with a client, we shut down and lose the sale because we're reacting to some disappointment we lived through with another entirely unrelated client. We run from a chance to make more money, because our family upbringing taught us to fear and avoid it—even though we would *say* we want more of it. The list goes on.

When you don't know your own Story, the pivot points on which your life turns, your unexamined emotions are left to steer the ship while the captain sleeps. They'll steer you right into a hurricane or even create a drama-filled storm of their own, blowing your dreams off-course and even self-sabotaging your success—all without your knowing what caused the disaster in the first place.

And let's face it. We don't have to look too far or listen too much to find examples of all the negative programming we've picked up along the way. As you go about life in the office or at home, do you ever hear stuff like:

- No one appreciates me for me
- I'm always the last to know
- It's not fair
- That's not in my job description
- I can't...
- We've always done it that way
- It's too late for me to change
- Life isn't fair
- No one wants to hear my opinion
- You'll never make a living at _____
- Why would you choose to do _____?
- You should be more like _____

That's all negative programming wired into us at some point or another, mostly without our ever realizing it. The reality is that most people are not even aware of the power of their words or the thoughts behind them. And they're almost certainly clueless as to how their Story shaped those thoughts in the first place. The same is probably true for you, just as it is for me.

What negative scripting have you picked up from your own Story without realizing it? What have you learned from your life experiences? Has that learning been helpful or harmful? What programming is your brain already subconsciously following?

All the negative scripting also illustrates just the opposite: the power of the positive messages you've received in life. Think back to those kind or encouraging words that stuck with you from long ago, that still drive you forward to this day in your darkest hour. All of it shapes who you are.

It's not enough to simply know your DNA hardwiring and live that out. That's a good start, but it's only part of the process of building your authenticity. As we live life and interact with others, we develop learned behaviors that help us navigate through relationships, handle failure and disappointments and create successes.

Your experiences have taught you learned behaviors that determine how you apply your hardwired uniqueness, or in some cases, don't apply your uniqueness. These learned behaviors shape your Story just as your DNA hardwiring does. Perhaps you touched a hot stove as a child and learned not to do that again. That's a good thing. But perhaps you leaned into your strengths in a meeting at work and got shot down—and said *I'll never do that again.* You crawled back into The Success Box, and your brilliance hasn't been seen since. Both reactions are understandable, but one can keep you safe, while the other can create incredible stress, frustration, and a hole inside that drains the life right out of you.

Often we pick up these behaviors unintentionally. We are all built with strong mechanisms for self-preservation. Sometimes that helps us make better decisions that are healthy and good for us. But many times it can cause us to make decisions driven by short-term "preservation" at the expense of long-term detriment.

When we experience something painful or traumatic, self-preservation kicks in and changes us to some extent. If we allow these changes to take root and grow, it will significantly alter who we are, for better or worse. The trick is to recognize it, seek to understand the emotion of it, and then leverage it to add another positive dimension to your life. Easier said than done. Most of the time we simply react and adjust to get through the situation without any thought of how it can magnify your greatness.

We instinctively choose a safer path. We try to move on without revisiting the discomfort. That's not all bad. The reality is that we're wired to forget. We need to if we're going to survive. The world can be a painful place, and neither our ancestors nor us would be much good if we couldn't forget stuff and move on. Our brain actively protects us from dwelling on things that might appear harmful. But when we ignore our Story, we fail to learn how it might be influencing us without our even realizing it. We don't intentionally choose our best path; we simply drift. But once we've moved on, it's important to reflect and reexamine the events of our lives, so we can gain a consciousness of how our power has been expanded through it all.

Not reflecting and examining can have one of two effects. We can become negative and toxic, similar to Louis Zamperini, or we can decide to be weird in a positive way, the same way Zamperini did once he stopped and faced his past head on. It is our pain and struggles, when intentionally evaluated, that can lead us to do our greatest good.

> It is our pain and struggles, when intentionally evaluated, that can lead us to do our greatest good.

Accidental Heroes

Your life's experiences are as unique as your DNA. Your Story includes all of the world you've experienced with joy and pain, success and failure, beauty and ugliness. Every joyous or agonizing detail adds dimension to your uniqueness and—*don't miss this*—contributes to your brilliance.

Gail Larsen, author of *Transformational Speaking: If You Want to Change the World, Tell a Better Story* says, "When you begin to understand the heroic nature of your own life journey, you'll find archetypal lessons that can inspire others to triumph over obstacles. Most of us are accidental heroes."[14] How true that is!

In my work with leaders of organizations, I help them discover their authenticity and to create an authentic culture within their company. I hear amazing stories from leaders who have overcome tremendous adversity, pain, and setbacks. And time and again, I discover each of those individuals wouldn't trade those painful experiences for anything. They've come to realize that all of it has shaped their Story and positioned them to be phenomenal leaders. In fact, it's often the most painful parts of their lives that produced the greatest growth.

Failure and having things not go your way can actually be the fertilizer for your success. Some of the most successful people failed before they succeeded. Walt Disney was fired for "lacking imagination." Oprah Winfrey was fired because she became too invested in her stories. Steven Spielberg tried and failed, multiple times, to get accepted to the USC School of Cinematic Arts. Colonel Sanders was in his mid-60s before Kentucky Fried Chicken became a success. Thomas Edison's teachers famously told him he was "too stupid to learn anything." And J.K. Rowling was a single mom living on welfare when she had the idea to write a book about a boy wizard named Harry Potter.

What they all learned is that life seldom follows our plans. A friend of mine says, "Life is all about how you handle plan B." Life unfolds in an unpredictable fashion, but the richness of life's lessons become the foundation of our purpose. That foundation is made of life events such as bankruptcy, death, divorce, abuse, business disasters, health problems, and a host of other painful things. It is also built upon love, the birth of a child, an act of kindness from someone you didn't know, the thrill of a huge business success, and other joyous life experiences.

I used to think that no one wanted to hear about my painful mistakes or the bad things that have happened in my Story. What I discovered is quite the opposite. Those painful experiences are common elements that bind us together. When we share our stories in vulnerability, we find community. We find connection. We find that we are not alone on the journey. Most importantly, if we're intentional about re-engaging those painful parts of our Story, we can actually extract value from those life-shaping experiences.

Think about that: your most painful season of life may actually be what positions you to deliver something incredibly and uniquely valuable. Now, that's weird. But it's true.

> Your most painful season of life may actually be what positions you to deliver something incredibly and uniquely valuable.

Perhaps a painful chapter from my own weird Story will illustrate how all of these ups and downs can create powerful life-defining experiences.

The year was 2007. I was in my 11th year of building a substantial and successful real estate business. My company was involved in real estate brokerage, sales and marketing of residential communities, and development of residential and commercial projects. I was doing multi-million dollar deals all the time.

Sometimes I would touch a project for only a couple months and walk away with hundreds of thousands of dollars. It wasn't unusual to make one phone call and raise several million dollars from investors to do a new deal. Banks were my best friend and willing to offer multi-million dollar loans for just about any project. The real estate business was good. Life was good.

And then it happened, the infamous real estate crash that eventually led to the most significant financial collapse in the United States since the Great Depression. We saw the collapse of Lehman Brothers, Bear Stearns, and many of the country's largest banks.

It was not a pretty picture, and my Story was smack in the middle of it all. I had millions of dollars of real estate loans that I had personally guaranteed—and no possible way to pay them back. No one was buying real estate, but I was carrying millions of dollars worth of projects. For the next two years, to say my life unraveled would be an understatement. Events went from bleak, to bad, to unthinkable. No money coming in. Lots of money going out. No way to satisfy the banks. The banks constantly cranking up the pressure. Lawsuits flew. Assets evaporated.

Every day I woke up convinced that nothing good was going to happen. During one two-week stretch, I threw up every morning to start my day. All news was bad news and nothing I did helped. I watched all that I had worked for my entire life disappear. The pressure was so heavy that I was almost completely paralyzed by it. I lost any sense of who I was and felt utterly worthless. In what seemed to be an instant, I had gone from successful entrepreneur to a middle-aged man with no future.

I remember one evening, however, that changed everything for me. As I stood in the kitchen with my wife, I began to share with her just how bad things were. In my own pride, I had tried to shield her from the severity of the situation. But that night, I shared it all. I told her we were flat broke and probably about to lose our house.

Through the tears and intense sense of shame, I apologized for allowing this to happen and told her I was sorry for failing her and our family. I told her the guy that always seemed to make things work, the guy she could always depend on, was out of ideas: "Sweetheart, I have no idea what to do." I was broken, hopeless, and struggling simply to breathe.

I had no idea at the time, but what happened next proved to be a pivotal moment in my Story, putting me on the path to finding my true purpose. What she said left me speechless. It was a catalyst for adding a new dimension to who I am, resulting in such a powerful experience that the changes are ingrained in me as much as into my biological DNA. I came to see those painful circumstances as a necessary step in defining WHO I am.

Taking Back Your Future

So how do you do that? How do you go about making sense of it all—what has happened to you, the choices you've made, and all the things outside of your control—and start intentionally shaping your own destiny? I know, some of you are wondering what it was my wife said that changed everything for me. Not to worry, I'll share the rest of that Story a little farther in our journey together. But first let's explore how to reclaim your Story.

Certainly, it helps to have a guide, someone who can give you an unbiased, objective perspective. As an executive coach, I walk through this process with high-performers all the time. But I can't be everywhere (I'm not that weird!), and sometimes we need to seek other professionals to help us navigate what we find (therapists, spiritual leaders, counselors, etc).

So here is the simple, three-part process I suggest:

Look Back. Schedule time to reflect on your life journey. You'll need to block this time and protect it so you can truly ask and answer deeper questions like these:

- ⮑ What is your most beloved childhood memory and why?
- ⮑ What people most influenced your growth? Parents,teachers, coaches, bosses, mentors, etc.?
- ⮑ What events caused a change in your life direction, for better

or worse? Don't think the events need to be huge. They can be, but often it's seemingly smaller things that shifted our thinking and redirected our paths.

- What dreams did you once have for your life that you set aside along the way and why?
- What have been your highest highs? You lowest lows? What changed in your Story as a result?

Look Around. After looking back, it's time to evaluate where you are now in your Story. Answering questions like these will help get you started: What is your most beloved childhood memory and why?

- What am I doing now in my life and career that is very positive *because of* those previous influences?
- On the other hand, what am I doing now in my life and career that is negative *because of* those previous influences?
- How "in control" do I feel about the life I am living right now?
- What people and influences are shaping my Story the most in my current season of life? Are those influences positive or negative?
- What is going into my mind now that is shaping my own programming for better or worse?
- If you were a friend of yourself, would you want to hang out with you? Why or why not? (The truth is that some of us are the epitome of gracious to others, but real jerks to ourselves, often as result of previous experiences and negative programming. We beat ourselves up every day then wonder why we don't see the greatness within.)
- How do I talk to and about myself in this season of life?
- What am I choosing to tolerate in my life right now and why?

Look Forward. You have the power to shape your own destiny, my friend. Once you look back and around, it's time to set your sites on the future. You don't control everything, of course, but you do control your direction and how you respond to what has happened to you.

- Where do you want to go? Do you know? You can't shape your destiny if you don't know your *destin*-ation. If you don't know your destination, then any road will do. No one ever accidentally maximized their greatness.

- What values will guide you on your journey ahead? We'll delve more into this important piece in the next chapter. For now, what comes to mind as the non-negotiable core values you want to define your Story going forward?

- How can you leverage what has happened to you to fulfill your own purpose in a weird way that reveals your greatness to the world?

- What destructive habits need to be replaced with positive habits in order to take control of your Story and shape your destiny?

- How committed are you to fully realizing the greatness within and sharing it with the world in a way that multiplies your impact and influence?

- How will you intentionally remain aware of the impact of your Story to keep those pivotal moments from fading as you encounter new experiences?

- What is the essence of that weirdness (or wyrd-ness) that empowers you to shape your destiny?

You could ask a lot more questions because your own assessment will be as unique as you are. But this will get you started in the *weird* direction. I also suggest you write these things down and examine them. Be honest with yourself, but don't be too hard on yourself. The truth is, you have more power to control your Story than you may think.

For those of you still struggling to believe you have the power to shape your own destiny, Zig Ziglar often asked these 4 simple but powerful questions to help strip away the excuses:

1. Do you believe there is something you can do that will make your life worse?
2. Do you believe there is something you can do that will make your life better?
3. Do you believe the choice is yours?
4. Do you believe every choice has an end result?

If you answered *yes* to each of those 4 questions—and it's awfully hard not to—what you are saying is: Bad things may have happened to you, but you don't have to let the "victim" label define you. In fact, those "bad things" may have shaped you into a better, more powerful person, driven to deliver your unique blend of greatness to the world. Fate need not have its way with you. It's time to leave the past where it belongs, behind you. Learn from it? Absolutely. Let it control you? Absolutely not! You can choose to do something right now that will make your future better and brighter. It's up to you!

That's really weird thinking these days. Being intentional about understanding and shaping your Story is not normal. But remember— greatness is not normal. You are a unique and wonderful human being. You must recognize the impact of your choices. Only then can you have clarity to choose the Story you will write moving forward.

You can't change the past… but you can learn from it and choose to shape your future. The weird ones—the great ones—always do.

You can't change the past… but you can learn from it and choose to shape your future. The weird ones—the great ones—always do.

Chapter 8

Your Values

> "When your values are clear to you, decisions become easier." — Roy E. Disney

January 31, 1990: another bitterly cold morning in Moscow. But that day, instead of bustling about, 35,000 Soviet citizens were lined up for miles down the street. What were they waiting for? An event many expected they would never see: the grand opening of Russia's very first McDonald's.

Executives were elated when, after twenty years of finagling, they finally secured government permission to raise the golden arches over Moscow. Seating up to nine hundred guests at once, and sporting twenty-seven speedy registers, the restaurant was ready for anything. Well, almost anything.

Not only did the food chain represent American capitalism and quick-service culture, but also McDonald's had been running on a certain set of values that turned out to be the opposite of what their new employees knew. It started with *smiles*.

American retail and dining culture has become known for that slogan, "The customer is always right." For better or for worse, it has become the waiter/clerk's job to satisfy potential buyers, usually with a positive attitude, helpful conversation, and lots of *smiles*.

Politeness towards strangers, however, even towards customers, wasn't a value that Russians were commonly taught. In fact, in the era of Soviet rationing, those with access to food, money or products held all of the power over the ones wanting to acquire them. Food would take hours to come out. If the staff didn't feel like serving, they could shoo people away or claim that their nearly-empty restaurant just didn't have room.

And you *never* smiled at people you didn't know. Smiling was a vulnerable gift shared only with your close friends and family. In fact, the ubiquitous "American Smile" was thought of as deceptive and disconcerting among Russians. Why would a person smile that much? A stranger's grin meant they knew something about you they shouldn't, something they might even use against you.

So, understandably, this new value—the value of friendliness to the public—didn't come naturally to the 600 new employees. When they first applied for the job, they never expected to be introduced to a totally new way of seeing the world. But the McDonald's administration felt convinced that they could learn these new values. Training was held for hours, with videos of American employees—dubbed over in Russian of course—greeting customers with "How are you today?" and "How can I help you?"

At first the words felt strange. Holding eye contact was awkward and unexpected. But after the grand opening, as these men and women exercised their new social value, a curious thing happened. People loved it! People came in for food, but they also came in just to hang out. The atmosphere was different than anywhere else they had been—and the smiles were contagious! One employee went so far as to call it an island of light and humanity.[15]

A seemingly simple change in values changed an entire community. They had the same DNA as ever, the same hard-wiring, the same abilities and talents—but when their values changed, so did their actions, their motivations, and so did their success.

Two Types of Values

You didn't get to pick your natural talents and abilities. You were born into the weirdness of your DNA hardwiring. Your Story, however is a mix of actions and consequences, and choosing how to respond to what comes your way. You didn't choose all of your life experiences, but you did choose many of them and your response to them. It's the examination of both the choices and your responses that leads to valuable self-awareness.

And at first glance, your values might appear to be entirely your choice. However, the reality is that your values can be best understood by thinking of them in two distinct groups: your DNA Values and your Story Values.

News Flash! You don't get to choose all of your values. Some of them were chosen for you at birth. These DNA Values are hardwired into you just like your physical DNA and natural personality and behavioral tendencies. Because of your natural hardwiring, you will always value certain things more than others. For example, the introvert will always value time to recharge while the extrovert will always value connecting with other people. You cannot change these values, but you can be aware of them and manage them when interacting with others.

Both sets of values are deeply entrenched in who you are, yet they come from different sources. Your DNA values are those values you have as a result of how you are naturally wired. Like your DNA hardwiring, you can't really change them, although you can learn to control them to some degree once you're aware of them. But

> **Values are hardwired into you just like your physical DNA and natural personality and behavioral tendencies.**

under stress, your go-to values will emerge just as your hardwired go-to behaviors do.

For example, if you are hardwired to be highly methodical, structured, and precision-oriented, what will you naturally tend to value? Information, details, structure. Now, you may choose instead to value spontaneity, generalities, and creative mess, but it will always feel inauthentic and forced to you and those around you. Most importantly, you will never be all that good at it, and you'll end up really off course.

For me, I am wired to be spontaneous and take action; consequently, I value movement and getting things done. When I re-organize my office every January, I know my desk will be a creative space by March, because neat and orderly is not how I am wired to perform at my best. Your DNA hardwiring shapes some of your values, but not all.

Your Story or life experiences dramatically shape your other values. Here you have a lot more choices. Once again, though, your values are influenced, though not determined, by events and circumstances outside of yourself. Suppose you were brought up in a loving family where everyone was transparent about their feelings. You may have disagreed at times, but at the end of the day, everyone knew you would love each other. As a result, you're more likely to value openness and transparency in your relationships.

On the other hand, if you were raised in an emotionally stifled home, or even an abusive environment, you'll naturally struggle to value emotional authenticity and deep, high-trust relationships. Or you may be determined not to live your life like that anymore, and you'll value the open display of emotion and affection within your family. Either way you go, it's your choice, but unavoidably influenced by your life's experiences. This again reinforces the value of why you must be aware of, and come to terms with, your own Story.

In my own Story, for example, one of my top values is faith. My parents had me in church every time the doors were open. Today I make the choice to actively embrace that faith, but there is no doubt my Story shaped the likelihood of that happening. I shared one of my significant business and life struggles in the last chapter. As a result of that experience, I value connecting with and investing in people going through a similar season of life. I don't have to do it, but I choose to do so, largely because of my own Story.

Your Story Values are not right or wrong, per se. They are driven by your life experiences and ultimately determined by the values you *choose* to embrace.

Decision-Making Filters

How would you respond if I called you right now and said I've got the deal of a lifetime? It will make you a ton of money. There's proven demand for this product and established pipelines to supply it. We can't miss! I want us to go into business together selling crack cocaine. At that point, are you likely to ask questions like, *What's the cost of investment? Do you have a marketing plan? Have you established a distribution network and can you give me a demographic profile of our ideal customer?*

I doubt it. I'm hoping it wouldn't take long for you to turn me down. You might even hang up on me. Why? Because it wouldn't align with your values. Our values serve as "decision-making filters" that influence our choices. You are constantly using your values to sift through inputs to determine how you act and react to situations and circumstances. Your DNA comes with blind spots. Your Story colors your perceptions. Your Values serve as decision-making filters.

Let me share a few examples to illustrate the point. Let's suppose I am a highly challenging, action-oriented, candid person who operates well in conflict, and one of my direct reports is a harmonious, warm, and compassionate person with a high level of patience and a low tolerance for conflict and debate. When I attempt to engage in a healthy debate, my harmonious counterpart may become overly agreeable—even if they have a different opinion, because they value harmony more than they value voicing their viewpoint. I may discount any contribution they make to the conversation, because I

Your Values serve as decision-making filters.

value a hard-charging, challenging conversation and may view their harmonious nature as not being committed and lacking passion.

Perhaps you are wired for community and you value time socializing and collaborating with other people. It stimulates your creativity and gives you boundless energy. How well will you do if the company moves you to an isolated environment where you have to work independently for weeks on end? Not very well, because you value interaction and social activity.

If you are married, you can probably relate to this one. Maybe your spouse is more outgoing and loves to be at a party, a dinner, or any other place that gets them out of the house. You would prefer to stay in, eat dinner, and binge watch your favorite Netflix original series in the comfort of your PJs. When an opportunity comes to get out of the house, you may run it through your decision-making filter and decide you don't value that opportunity. You also may run it through your decision-making filter and decide that you value your spouse and marriage more than Netflix, so you decide to go out.

If you don't have clarity on your values, you have no clear framework with which to make decisions about work and life. Your values give you the compass to live out your Story with authenticity. They also keep you grounded, but you need to have a high level of self-awareness of your values and your definition of those values. You can't simply choose vague labels.

For example, when I sat down with my wife and boys to choose our family values, we decided integrity was going to be one of our Cagle values. "Boys, we have to define this," I challenged them. "What does it mean?" I'm proud to say that if you asked my sons what integrity means to the Cagles, they would say without hesitation, "Integrity is doing the right thing for the right reasons."

I saw this need to clarify values manifest itself in a powerful way once when working with a team of executive leaders. We had a great day rolling as we worked through this process. The team was tight-knit group who had worked together for many years and knew each other pretty well—or so they thought. As part of a values-clarification exercise, each leader shared a key value he or she had identified as being in his or her top five. As they went around the room, we heard things like *sense of urgency, loyalty, excellence,* and *integrity.* But then one guy, I'll call him Bill, shared something unexpected: money. The room erupted in guffaws and good-natured ribbing: ""You greedy bastard. It's all about money for you isn't it!" "Sure, Bill... Show me the money!" "I know what to get you for your birthday— cold, hard cash!" and on and on. As I said, they were all friends, so he took it well.

As the room quieted, I asked, "So tell us Bill, why is *money* a top value for you?" As he shared the reason behind his value, the room got really quiet.

"When I was growing up," Bill started, then paused to swallow before continuing, "there was one time of year I dreaded—when it was time to go back to school after summer break. All the other parents took their kids to buy new school clothes and shoes. All the kids came to school dressed in the latest fashion, but I wore my cousin's hand-me-downs. My jeans were tattered. My shoes were scuffed. All the kids would make fun of me. I was nicknamed 'Patches.' So I made a promise to myself that my daughters will never wear their cousin's clothes to school."

His peers, who were ragging on him just a few minutes earlier, went completely silent. Bill's value of money was his choice, but his choice was influenced by an experience in his life.

Bill knew what he valued. He defined what it meant to him. That clarity motivated him and gave him purpose. Most importantly, deep emotional connections from his Story fueled how he went about applying his unique brilliance. In fact, that value determined the goals he set, not the other way around. I suppose it's no surprise that he also served as the CFO.

Many people choose a goal in life, then try to reshape themselves to achieve it. Now, to be candid, it's not all their fault. Many times, they're coached wrong by well-meaning guides who start by asking, "What's your goal?" Then follow up with, "Great! Now let's put a 10-year plan in place to achieve it." But if you haven't first gotten in touch with who you are and what you value—your why—your pursuit of the goal will likely leave you frustrated and unfulfilled. Your natural hardwiring is where you get your energy, if you stay within the power of your natural gifts. But it's your Story that fuels the passion to sustain your efforts to achieve your goals and purpose.

Your goal may sound great:

- ➲ To be a partner in a law firm
- ➲ To be a *New York Times* bestselling author
- ➲ To make it to the C-suite
- ➲ To build a business from scratch
- ➲ To lead a non-profit organization
- ➲ To achieve an athletic goal

But few people ever stop to ask the important questions: Is this really the best fit for WHO you are? Will you really bring unique value if you achieved your goal, or would both you and others be better served by your pursuing a different goal? It's not as if you get a second shot at this thing called life. I've seen it again and again while working closely with successful people at every level. They climb the ladder only to realize it was leaning against the wrong building—and they can't get those years back.

Comedian Jim Carrey famously did this very thing by writing himself a check for $10 million dollars for "acting services rendered." He posted the check 3 years out and put it in his wallet and forgot about it. For Carey, the check symbolized the success he valued in a very specific way for what he was passionate about doing. Then he went work to live out what he valued by setting goals and achieving them. If he had started with "How do I make money?" he would never have connected with why it was so important. But because he started with who, his why drove him to figure out how to go about it and what exactly to do. (By the way, three years later, almost to the day, Carrey found out he landed the role of Lloyd in the movie *Dumb and Dumber*, and would receive $10 million for acting services rendered.)

Define your values first. Set goals second. And always ask this question: *Because of who I am, where do I want to go?*

> # Always ask this question: Because of who I am, where do I want to go?

Values Flex Over Time

Values are not static, by the way. Your values can and probably should change over time, depending on your season of life. For example, twenty years ago legacy was not one of my top values. It is today. Unlike our DNA, values evolve. If you're new to leadership, for example, you probably should value listening and absorbing wisdom from leadership veterans, asking for input more than taking action based on your instincts. But as you mature in your leadership growth, you'll likely develop an innate awareness of the "right" things to do in given situations. If you're intentional, you'll learn to lean into your DNA, recognize the influence of your experiences, and value taking the first step rather than waiting for others to give you direction.

Great athletes excel at discipline and healthy habits. They listen to their bodies and change their values over time to match what they need to thrive. Multiple reports suggest that Lebron James spends into the seven figures each year just on his body. He has a team of experts who help him compete at a peak level, including a former Navy SEAL who serves as his biomechanist, a strength and recovery coach, the team trainers with the Cleveland Cavaliers, and chefs and masseuses. In his home, he has a full gym, hot tub, ice tub, and hyperbaric chamber.[16] This is a man who values physical fitness, and the results speak for themselves. As of this writing he has appeared in 8 straight NBA finals, and after 15 years in the league is performing at what most commentators would say is his very best. Peak performance is clearly something he values. His value choice is informed by his DNA (including his physical makeup) and his Story.

Another athletic example would be Tiger Woods. By his own admission, he struggled after his father's death.[17] His Story went into the weeds. He suffered from debilitating back pain. His marital struggles are well-documented. All of it contributed to bringing him to a place where he had to readdress his values. The good news is that by all accounts, he has chosen to redefine those values in a positive way with sources close to him saying he is looser, more engaging with fans, and mentoring younger golfers. The values he seems to be embracing now are different from those he chose when he first stormed onto the fairways twenty years ago.

The same truths apply outside the wide world of sports. Nelson Mandela valued equality late in his life, regardless of the color of a person's skin. Steve Jobs valued design and innovation. Jimmy Carter values helping people get into a home of their own. Even Louis Zamperini "valued" revenge after his ordeal as a prisoner of war, and then he later came to value forgiveness.

If you're a parent, you know this to be true—values change over time. Great parents sacrifice and do what needs to be done because they value their children and their children's future. Often times, parents set their own values aside for a season to focus on their children. They want to give their kids every chance at future success, so they pour into them in the early parts of their lives. As kids get older and take on more responsibility, parents can adjust back to their own values.

How to Identify Your Values

Using this simplified process is an easy way to get your values discovery process underway. However, it's important to remember that it takes time to put all the pieces together. I typically invest 6-7 months with coaching clients to dive deep into discovering DNA, Story, and Values, and then, most importantly, helping them intentionally connect the dots to present the very best of their unique brilliance to the world.

A straightforward way to identify your DNA values is to examine each of the 6 Ways You're Wired to Be Weird. Look at the lists of DNA values that follow and choose the one that resonates the most with you:

When it comes to CONTROL, I naturally value...

Accommodating

Process
Speaking tactfully
Cooperation
Practical concerns
Focused activity
Cautious response

Directing

Getting results
Speaking directly
Initiating action
Future clarity
Competitive challenges
Proactive behavior

Your leading DNA Value for CONTROL: _____

When it comes to INTERACTION, I naturally value...

Reserved

Realistic
Perseverance
Focus
Analysis
Productivity
Closure

Engaging

Enthusiasm
Optimism
Flexibility
Recognition
New people
Energy

Your leading DNA Value for INTERACTION: _____

When it comes to CONFLICT AND PACE, I naturally value...

Challenging

Cool objectivity
Taking action
Responding quickly
Difficult decisions
Change
Logical analysis

Harmonious

Compassion
Patience
Stable consistency
Loyalty
Feelings
Careful listening

Your leading DNA Value for CONFLICT AND PACE: _____

When it comes to ORDER, I naturally value...

Spontaneous

Flexibility
Big picture
Improvisation
Instinctive action
On-the-spot decisions
Candid directness

Methodical

Organized scheduling
Accurate details
Effective systems
Analysis-driven decisions
Research
Diplomatic responses

Your leading DNA Value for ORDER: _____

When it comes to ADVENTUROUSNESS, I naturally value...

Cautious

Avoiding risk
Balanced life
Building consensus
Moving cautiously
Voice of reason

Adventurous

New challenges
Taking risks
Achieving goals
New opportunities
Optimism

Your leading DNA Value for ADVENTUROUSNESS: _____

When it comes to INNOVATION, I naturally value...

Concrete

Practical solutions
Experience
Consistency
Solving problems
Identifying pitfalls
Concrete issues

Abstract

Abstract thinking
Multiple perspectives
Creative imagination
New approaches
Being resourceful
Mental challenges

Your leading DNA Value for INNOVATION: _____

In addition to your hardwired DNA Values, you have Story Values that are shaped by your life experiences. Your family history, defining moments, personal beliefs, and life choices all work together to guide the values you choose to embrace. Unfortunately, few people pause long enough to clearly identify those values and be consciously guided by them. They also keep you grounded, but you need to have a high level of self-awareness of your values and your definition of those values. You can't simply choose vague labels.

Look at the list of values below and begin thinking about what is most important to you. Feel free to add more that better fit your Story. Then circle the top twelve that immediately stand out. Then, cut the list to six. This exercise is supposed to make you think, so don't be surprised if it gets more difficult as you go.

Once you have your list down to six, you'll have a pretty clear sense of what you value and where it ranks in terms of importance to you.

Accountability	Enjoyment	Money/Wealth
Achievement	Fairness	Passion
Authority	Faith/Religion	Perfection
Balance	Family	Quality
Change	Fitness	Recognition
Commitment	Fun	Simplicity
Competence	Growth	Status
Courage	Honesty	Structure
Creativity/Innovation	Independence	Teamwork
Customer Satisfaction	Integrity	Trust
Diversity	Knowledge	Urgency
Effectiveness	Legacy	Volunteerism/Service
Efficiency	Loyalty	Wisdom

Now put these Story values together with your DNA values to get a clear picture of the filters you use to make your decisions in life and business.

Once you get clear on who you are by understanding your Big 3, that's only the beginning of the fun. Are you still with me? I hope so, because I'm about to show you the magic that is possible when you learn how to be weird—to tap into the power of you in a way that supercharges your success and sets up the rest of the world to make the most of your greatness.

Now, I've got to warn you, it isn't always easy to be weird, which is why most people don't do it. They settle for normal. They wait for the elevator instead of choosing to take the stairs. But the elevator to success is broken, as Zig Ziglar put it.[18]

I can see that's not you. If you've made it this far with me, you're obviously serious about making the most of your life. You're ready to be part of the Be Weird clan.

So let's do this! Let's explore together the second most important step in this Be Weird journey: how to leverage your brilliance in a way that protects your authenticity, multiplies your influence, and reveals very best of you to the world!

Chapter 9

What's Holding You Back from Being You?

"It's always better to try a swan dive and deliver a colossal belly flop than to step timidly off the board while holding your nose." — Jennifer Reingold

"Every block of stone has a statue inside it, and it is the task of the sculptor to discover it." So said Michelangelo, and it's the same with you. Discovering more about the work of art you are requires intentionally and carefully stripping away layers of life that have concealed your true beauty. Instead of running from struggles and flaws, you can learn to value them, just as a diamond is more valuable because of its defects. A man-made diamond is flawless, but not nearly as valuable as a natural diamond with all its flaws and imperfections created under intense pressures. So it is with people. Our true beauty lies in how we manage our imperfections, not in how well we pretend to be perfect.

I'd like to share a deeply personal story of a highly successful businessman. Today he is confident and bold, so you'd never suspect he once struggled to believe a positive future was possible. He was once a confused and disillusioned 13-year-old boy growing up in rural America.

On any given day, most people who knew him would have called him "troubled." The rest of the time, he was just that "bad kid" no one wanted hanging out with their own children. He didn't get invited to overnight parties or birthday bashes. In short, he was the kid parents warned theirs about. And everyone knew it. The consensus was that there was no hope for this young man. His future was set—and it looked pretty bleak. He presumed jail time would likely be part of his Story.

One day, after more disruptive behavior that left everyone shaking their heads, he was called to the principal's office. It wasn't his first visit; in fact, it seems he was a frequent visitor.

But on that day, the principal said something to the boy that had the power to shape the young man's destiny: "Son, there are people in this world that are just bad apples and everything they touch becomes rotten. You need to understand that you're one of them. Those bad apples don't contribute much to society. They're really not ever going to amount to anything."

The teen soaked it all in as the principal got to his main reason for the conversation: "I think you should consider doing yourself and the school a favor and just drop out of school. You're not learning anything. Being here isn't going to help you, because you just don't care."

This wasn't the first time the boy had heard stuff like that—*You're no good. You'll never amount to anything.* But for some reason, those words hit close to his heart that day. His mind went to some pretty dark places that no teen mind should ever go. Fortunately, the story didn't end that day.

A few days later, when he showed up for science, the teacher asked to see him after class. The boy sighed as he sat down across from yet another desk, wondering why he hadn't taken the principal's advice and stayed home—or worse. No doubt he racked his brain, trying to think what he had done this time to earn another lecture. But this conversation took a very different path.

She started with a bombshell: "I couldn't let this day go by without telling you something. I don't see you the way other people see you." The surprised boy perked up. "There's something different about you. There's a value inside you that is different and unique." *Unique.* That was a word he had never heard used in reference to himself. Shocked, he leaned in as she continued. "I don't know what it is exactly, but if you want, I'll help you find it."

At that moment, the boy was skeptical, wondering if his principal and this teacher were conspiring to trick him in some way. He had never heard anything like it. And even though he was sure the offer was a ploy with some hidden motive, he decided he couldn't resist the offer.

For the first time in his life, the "troubled" boy began to believe that he had a future. He began to believe that he had something *valuable and unique* to contribute to the rest of the world. At first he resisted, but as the teacher began authentically delivering on her promise, his hope began to grow and override his cynicism. As her authenticity built trust with the boy, she walked alongside him for the next several years. As a result, that troubled boy went from nearly dropping out of school—and life—to graduating near the top of his class.

If you would have told that boy who left the principal's office that he would go on to start several successful companies, employ hundreds of people, and work with some of the most successful people on the planet, he would have retorted, "You're smoking crack!"

Yet that is exactly what happened. But as I think about this story, I realize something powerful: that teacher was just being who she was wired to be. She was wired to work with kids. Her Story led her to that classroom that day. Did she have a defining moment in her own Story that contributed to her weirdness in a way that moved her to see something of value in that boy? For that boy, her conversation proved to be a defining moment in his Story that shaped his passion for believing in the potential of others and encouraging them to succeed.

Clearly, the teacher chose Story Values that moved her to care and believe in him when he had no belief of his own. When the principal wanted that boy gone, she attached herself to him, the rottenest kid in the school. And she did it naturally, because of who she was.

But don't miss this truth either: the principal who encouraged that boy to drop out probably thought at the time that he was doing what was best. Tough love. Discipline. Protect the other kids. Maybe in his past, the principal had experienced, and maybe even benefited from tough love from a father, grandparent, or another school leader. No doubt, he meant well, but he was really trying to cram that boy into his own version of The Success Box. The principal said, "I'm in charge. Straighten up or else. This is the way you need to be." The teacher said, "If you want, I'll help you learn about you." Big difference.

And in that one moment, the boy found the hope to overcome the doubts and fears that could have derailed his life Story forever.

The Greatest Accomplishment

Before I show you how to reposition your weird self in a way that brings the greatest fulfillment to you and most significant value to the world, we need to have a candid conversation about something—the never-ending pressures to compromise who you really are.

The poet Ralph Waldo Emerson put it best: "To be yourself in a world that is constantly trying to make you something else is the greatest accomplishment." How true is that!

> "To be yourself in a world that is constantly trying to make you something else is the greatest accomplishment."
> — Ralph Waldo Emerson

You know it to be true. You feel it every day, don't you? From the time you awake each morning until the time you fall into bed every night, you're told what you *should* be, how you *should* look, and what you *should* do.

Drive this car. Wear this brand. Fat is bad. Thin is good. Tan is good. Pale is bad. Hair is good. Bald is bad. White-collar is good. Blue-collar is failure (until you need your car repaired). College is required. Risk is bad. 401Ks are good. And so it goes.

However, when you look at the history of the world, or even the last few decades, the one constant is change. A couple centuries ago, women were encouraged to put on the pounds to be more attractive. Now they're often told that borderline anorexic is "beautiful." Wigs for men used to be a sign of respect and higher station in life. Now a shaved head is sexy. Becoming a tradesman and working with your hands used to be applauded as a noble line of work that any parents would be proud of their children for pursuing.

Workplaces used to be utilitarian and functional, now they are dynamic and fun. Women used to be all but banned from the boardroom, now some of the most successful companies in the world have female CEOs.

- And what about all the things "they" said will never happen?
- Man wasn't meant to fly. (December 17, 1903, Wilbur and Orville Wright left the ground in the first powered aircraft.)
- Man will never set foot on the moon. (July 20, 1969, "That's one small step for man, one giant leap for mankind.")
- No runner will ever break the 4-minute mile. (May 6, 1954, Roger Bannister runs a mile in 3:59:4.) As of this writing, 4,972 people have done it.
- "We don't like their sound, and guitar music is on the way out."[19] (Decca Recording Co. rejecting the Beatles, 1962.)
- No one can win 8 gold medals in a single Olympic games. (Michael Phelps did, Beijing 2008.)

Bottom line: all the expectations you're bombarded with every day can and do change. What *should* happen often *doesn't* happen.

So if you live your life trying to fit who you are into other people's expectations, your journey to maximize the power of you will be easily derailed.

It's not easy to stay authentic under this constant pressure. That's why I'm warning you right up front. Every day you have to choose to be you. Every day you have to look within to reconnect with who you really are. Every day you'll encounter resistance, both from outside influences and from within. You'll encounter "principals" who speak negative things into your life. You'll wrestle with doubts and struggle to muster up self-confidence. You'll ask yourself troubling questions: Am I really special? Do I dare believe that I could be, or already am, great? Sure, Greg thinks so, but what does he know? Maybe he's wrong.

> Every day you have to choose to be you.

But here's the thing, my friend. The struggle is worth it. *You* are worth it. The key is to protect against these negative voices. It won't be easy, but if you identify those potential *derailers* and face them head-on, you can keep them from shaping your destiny. As *New York Times* bestselling author Rory Vaden puts it, "Success is never owned. It is rented. And the rent is due every day."

5 Authenticity Killers

In my experience of working with high-performers across all walks of life, I'm continually amazed at how many seemingly successful people fall for myths about authenticity. These are authenticity killers that, if believed, will keep you from realizing your full potential.

Before we get into how to live out who you really are, we need to expose them right now so they don't derail you, too.

Myth #1. There's only one right way to do it.

Hands down, this is the single most destructive myth. I see it all the time. When we buy into it, our creative brain literally shuts down. After all, if there really is only one way to lead, for example, why would we ever think that living out our own unique style could work?

There are almost always many ways to do anything. Just because it has been done one way, doesn't mean it's the right way—or even the best way for you or your team to do it. In fact, just the opposite is true. When you try to achieve something in the same way others have done, you almost guarantee that you will never succeed. Why? Because you are not them. You are unique. You are brilliant in your own way. Thinking there is only one way strips you of your personal magic: your weirdness.

We see this truth play out all the time, though we often ignore it when it applies to ourselves. Think of the last five presidential elections

> Thinking there is only one way strips you of your personal magic: your weirdness.

at any time in history. Did any of them win by doing what everyone else did? No. Each winning candidate forged his own path. And those who tried to follow the "right way" were the ones who lost.

The same is true when you think about some of the greatest basketball players to ever play the game: think of Michael Jordan, Lebron James, and Larry Bird to name a few. All were MVP material. And yet each of them chose a path to success that was unique to their own talents and skills. Jordan could shoot, but was also one of the best defenders to ever play the game. Lebron is a scoring machine, but he can also bring the ball up the floor and dish out assists right and left. Larry Bird's basketball smarts and smart shooting left everyone in awe, but he couldn't jump like Jordan. Each achieved greatness by tapping into his own unique blend of talents. Had one tried to follow the path of the other, we'd likely never remember his name. The same is true across every sport, every industry, and every life.

Are there realities that each of us must work with and around? Certainly. And we'll get to that next. But squash this authenticity killer right now: the best way for you to succeed is your way.

Myth #2. If people really knew me, they wouldn't accept me.

We all want people to like us. We all want to be either accepted or respected—and often both. But remember what we discovered earlier: The gravitational pull to be accepted and respected is greater than the desire to be authentic and live out the real you.

Ironically, the secret to gaining greater acceptance and respect is to be more authentic to who you really are, not less. When we start with acceptance as the goal, we lose everything that makes us weird. And here's a startling truth: people are attracted to what makes us weird. That's right. There are people in the world right now that, if they knew who you really were, would flock to you. They would be excited that someone like you exists. They couldn't wait to connect with you.

> The gravitational pull to be accepted and respected is greater than the desire to be authentic.

We hear lots of talk these days about creating a following and building a tribe of raving fans. For most people, the plan looks like this: see what others are doing to get liked and copy them. But it doesn't work, because it's not real. Whatever success they do have will ultimately be unsustainable.

We all have it, no matter how much we want to deny it—this inner desire to be part of something, to be accepted, loved, and appreciated. We're willing to do almost anything for it.

However, the surest, most sustainable path to acceptance, appreciation, and respect—and, yes, love—is to let that love, acceptance, appreciation, and respect happen as a result of you being you. When you choose to start with authenticity, others benefit more from you. Your contribution to anything is magnified by a factor of ten when it comes from that place of your unique brilliance.

Recall how the fans responded to Babe Ruth's legendary home run that day in Boston. At least half the people in the stadium that day hated his guts for hitting those homers. They definitely did not accept him when he lived out who he was and became great. But everyone respected him. And over time, that respect turned into acceptance, as The Great Bambino is recognized as one of the greatest players ever to step on the field.

The reason we often fail to recognize this truth is that we're trying to gauge our worth by the expectations of those around us at the moment. However, when we try to conform to others' expectations, we unintentionally create distance between us and the very people we want to attract. Even if we can't put our finger on why, the gap grows over time.

Start with who you are, and love, acceptance, and respect will naturally follow.

Myth #3. Anyone could do what I do.

We could put this myth another way: I'm not really all that special. This self-talk script is so destructive, but it gets played repeatedly in our minds when fail to realize one simple truth: We naturally devalue our own brilliance.

There are things you are naturally wired to do better than anyone else. Your Story has shaped your capacity to excel in those areas. And your values position you to truly max it out. But because it comes so naturally to you, you don't realize how exceptional you really are. You think everyone could do what you do, if they wanted to. They just don't want to.

I've been fortunate to work with so many unique and wonderful people from all over the world, many of whom are extremely successful business leaders and entrepreneurs. Yet I am always amazed at how often they are completely unaware of their exceptional talents and brilliance. I've come to realize that we all tend to devalue our natural gifts and talents precisely because they are so valuable. Because they come so easily to us, we conclude those superpowers must be ordinary. But no one is you, and that is your superpower. So we go through our day-to-day lives pursuing things that are totally misaligned with our brilliance and power.

> **No one is you, and that is your superpower.**

For example, my weirdness lies in my natural DNA traits of curiosity, challenging, spontaneity, and adaptability, while my experiential Story influences are persistence, collaboration, encouragement, and empathy. All of these are framed by my values of faith, integrity, sense of humor, sense of urgency and legacy. When I draw from these and stay true to them, not only do I have greater impact, but also I feel exhilarated and tireless. I feel more fulfilled and am told by others around me that I inspire them.

However, in spite of my awareness of this myth, sometimes I fall into this trap of thinking that what comes easy to me can't possibly have value. I devalue my brilliance and try to be what I perceive to be more valuable or what my environment needs. In those instances, I feel exhausted, frustrated, and unfulfilled. I frustrate those around me and am constantly misunderstood.

Have you ever felt this? Does it happen way too often? Are you feeling it now? If so, you are operating outside of your weirdness.

This myth takes root at an early age when we're conditioned to fit in, not stand out. And yet you were designed to stand out. No one is like you. The world is not complete without you. Not the *you* everyone expects you to be. Not the *you* that tries to be who you think you need to be to succeed. The *real* you. The authentic *you*. You have far more value than you could possibly imagine. Mother Teresa put it so powerfully: "We ourselves feel that what we are doing is but a drop in the ocean. But the ocean would be less because of that drop."

Myth #4. Authenticity requires perfection.

Let's start debunking this myth with a little fact-checking truth: You are one of a kind. You've never existed before, and you'll never be duplicated again. It's not even debatable.

Every human being on the planet has a unique set of gifts and talents given at birth. The complex strands of our DNA provide us with something that can never be duplicated. No one is any more special than another, but each of us are one-of-a-kind and irreplaceable. Understanding who you are at your core, and embracing your perfections and imperfections is crucial to expressing your brilliance and its power. But being authentic and real doesn't mean you have to be perfect.

I once advised a talented and charismatic businesswoman. Everyone could see her talent. Many people admired and wanted to be more like her. I could easily see how she profoundly influenced others. And yet, she seemed to be in a constant state of restlessness, always striving to be something more.

To be candid, after working with her for several months, I became frustrated by her constant restlessness. No matter how much I tried to point out her power and brilliance, she seemed to always focus on her shortcomings and push herself towards what she called "self-improvement." Finally, one day as I thought about how best to help her more fully step into her greatness, I sent her this frank message:

I was thinking about you today and how I might help you realize the power of you. This is the thought that occurred to me. There is no need to be perfect to inspire those around you. People aren't inspired by perfection. They are inspired by how you deal with your imperfection. Your perfections are nice, but it's your imperfections that are inspiring.

It's good to want to get better; it's good to want to grow, but don't be so intensely focused on getting better that you miss the opportunities of *you* today. You may not be where you want to be, but you are powerful and inspiring now. I've seen how people react to you, and I see how many people aspire to be like you. Don't let that go without the impact it's meant to deliver.

Almost as soon as I sent the message, I realized that message applies to all of us. Regardless of where you are in your life right now, there is greatness within you. The power that is *you* exists in your perfections (yes, you have those) *and* in your imperfections. Remember, the diamond with imperfections is worth much more than the man-made, perfect diamond. The process of discovering and revealing the unique mix of perfections and imperfections is essential to unleashing your brilliance.

One of the greatest mistakes we can make is to think the qualities we need are "out there" somewhere and we need to go find them. The truth is that you already possess what makes you amazing, powerful, and brilliant.

Myth #5. Failure is fatal.

The feature film *Darkest Hour* brings to life Winston Churchill, that "British bulldog" I referred to at the beginning of our journey.[20]

The story focuses on Churchill's seemingly sudden ascent to power just as Hitler was invading and occupying most of the European mainland. Within weeks of his taking office as Prime Minister, Churchill faced a crushing dilemma through no fault of his own. As Hitler's forces pressed through France, more than 300,000 British troops, essentially the entire British army, had become stranded on the beaches of the English Channel—the French side of the channel. Surrounded by advancing Nazi forces, the British had no air support nor fleets available to sail in to rescue the troops.

All hope seemed lost. By all accounts, it was one of the most significant failures in British military history. Members of Churchill's War Cabinet pressured him to negotiate terms of surrender with Hitler. In their minds, and in the minds of his military leaders, the failure would prove fatal. His critics believed they should surrender and live to fight another day.

But while everyone else had given up, Churchill's bulldog DNA hardwiring, his Story of perseverance against tremendous odds, and his unwavering Values of patriotism and persistence moved him to choose a counterintuitive response: "Success is never final. Failure is never fatal. It is the courage to continue that counts."

> What would you attempt to do if you knew you could not fail?

As a result, Churchill initiated a historic effort against all odds to mobilize civilian vessels to transport the stranded troops across the Channel. In just eight days, more than 80 boats rescued 338,226 troops. Because he refused to accept failure as final, he persisted until he found a solution.

What about you? Do you fear failure? Worse, do you fear the laughter and ridicule that might result from your efforts falling short? Stop and ask yourself: Has your greatest fear ever really come true? Even if it has, did it lead to your demise? Failure is a part of your ongoing growth and evolution as a uniquely powerful human being.

I have a paperweight on my desk that asks me a question every time I sit down: *What would you attempt to do if you knew you could not fail?* How would you answer that question? How would the people in your organization answer that question? How about the leadership of your company?

First, let's come to terms with reality. Let's acknowledge your fears do have some merit. Failure will happen, and it has does have consequences, although they are seldom as bad as we imagine them to be.

So, perhaps the next question should be: how do you feel about failure? One mindset to take is that failure should not be feared, but managed. Minimize the risk of failure and make plans for when it happens. Doing so can keep fear paralysis from setting in.

An overblown fear of failure stifles creativity. It initiates a fight-or-flight response in the brain, leaving you literally unable to think straight. That fear-on-steroids effect eliminates healthy risk taking and causes a person to stay in their comfort zone instead of stepping out to explore their true passions.

Do you remember the story of my own business failure after the real estate crash of 2007? After building a wildly successful real estate business, the market collapsed. I was left personally responsible for millions of dollars of real estate loans. I had no way to pay them back. My life went from bad to worse to hopeless, and I threw up to start every day. Remember that? That's what failure feels like, my friend. Believe me, I've felt it.

You may still be wondering how that story ended. What did my wife say that changed everything for me in my own "darkest hour?" Well, I shared with her for the first time how truly bad it was— we were broke, and the bank was probably taking our house. As I apologized through the tears for having failed her and our family, I finally swallowed and said simply, "Sweetheart, I just don't know what to do."

What happened next left me speechless and still sends shivers up my spine today. She didn't hesitate in her response. She looked straight at me and said simply, "I don't know what to do either, but I'm married to you. And I believe in you. So I'm going to go bed and sleep."

At that moment, nothing changed—and everything changed. Tomorrow was going to be another day of hell, but somehow I suddenly believed I could get through it all.

Over the course of the next year, my Story experiences would add dimension to this life-defining moment. My best friend two houses down was going through an enormously difficult time also. He eventually lost his business and his home. He and I would sometimes stand in our driveway and talk until 3 in the morning. We cried together, suffered together, and we leaned on each other.

Another friend secured a loan and bought my house. He let me live there until I could get back on my feet. I eventually paid off the loan and sold my house for a profit. The pain of that life event is still with me. I still get emotional when telling the story. But through that painful chapter of my Story, I found opportunities to help other people who were struggling to find their way again in an authentic manner. Through that process, I discovered more of what I was truly wired to do—empower you to be you—and the seeds of this book were planted in my soul.

In that moment in the kitchen, I became a champion of the power of belief, although I didn't fully realize it at the time. I experienced the positive effect of it and became committed to believing in others, and inspiring them to believe in themselves.

I learned that I could apply my unique skills set and experiences to any number of industries and contribute value. I've been in the bar and restaurant business; I've been in the advertising industry; I've been in technology development, and I've been in the real estate business. As a result of my getting in touch with my own DNA and Story, I became an executive coach—talent maximizer—speaker and trainer—authenticity advocate–advisor to numerous companies of all sizes from family-run ventures to Fortune 100 companies to the Army Special Forces—success catalyst. All because I leaned into my Story and learned from it, painful though it was at the time.

Failure is not fatal. In fact, your failures are part of what make you brilliant and wildly weird. The road ahead won't be perfect… don't expect perfect. But there is good news. As entrepreneur Ryan Levesque says, "You don't have to get it perfect; you just have to get it going."[21]

Chapter 10

Presenting You to the World

The reason someone is remarkable is because
that person did something remarkable, and now that
remarkable thing is taken, and it's no longer remarkable
if you do it. Be weird. Do something remarkable.

When Benjamin Gates first discovered the Meerschaum pipe in the movie *National Treasure*,[22] he didn't realize the significance of the prize.

They pulled the pipe from a barrel of gunpowder in the frozen hold of a ship on their quest to discover that mother of all treasures. The pipe was an intricately carved, one-of-a-kind work of art depicting a castle scene complete with horse and rider. The handle contained a clue which led Gates and the rest of the treasure hunters to the map on the back of the Declaration of Independence. And that was all they thought it would give them, until much later, near the end of the story.

Only then did they discover the secret chamber beneath Trinity Church in New York City (thanks to the spectacles I referenced earlier). And only then did they realize that there was a hole in a wall that only that unique pipe could fill. But it wasn't enough to have the pipe fill the hole. It had to be inserted in just the right way. Then the handle of the pipe had to be applied in just the right manner to unlock and reveal the concealed treasure to the awestruck world.

And so it is with you. You see, it's not enough to simply uncover your own weirdness. That's where the journey must begin, for sure. Just like the intricate pipe was amazing in and of itself, its true purpose was revealed only when it filled the intended hole in just the right way. When you fill the hole in the universe that only you can fill, something truly magnificent is revealed to the world. I would even dare to say that something truly magical happens.

Now remember, we're not talking about merely becoming better than average. Nor are we talking about simply taking your performance to the next level. We're talking about greatness, the stuff of which legends are made. If greatness is our aim, we must rediscover it, unlock it, and then present our weirdness to the world in just the right way.

It's the combination of your uniqueness and the application that unleashes the power of you.

What Really Makes the Difference?

It's not enough to say, "Hey world! This is who I am. Take it or leave it. And frankly, I don't give a damn!" You may know someone who tried that approach. You may have even tried it yourself at times. How did that work out, for you? Not well, I'm guessing. That's because the old adage about fitting a round peg in a square hole is true; it doesn't work. Neither does yelling at the hole, expecting it to change to accommodate the peg. And, by the way, trying harder only damages both the peg and the hole.

No, to truly live out who you are with authenticity, you must learn how to present who you really are to the world in a way that positions you to make your highest contribution and, at the same time, invites others to live out who they are with authenticity as well.

So, I'm not talking about simply being *different*. That's a mistake a lot of people make, especially younger people who are full of energy but still short on experience. They confuse being different with being authentic. They turn to all sorts of external things to set themselves apart: a unique hairstyle, tattoos, body piercings, the latest fashion style (or just the opposite). They think that they become unique by changing how the world perceives them.

It's usually a well-intentioned step in the right direction. Those who've tried that approach figure out pretty quickly that, although they may feel better about themselves in the short-term, it's more difficult to grow their influence, increase their income, and have the significant impact they really desire. It takes more than that.

It's like Seth Godin says, "You cannot be remarkable by following someone else who's remarkable."[23] What makes you different makes you great—but only when it comes from a place of authenticity. Otherwise it just makes you a poser, an authenticity wanna-be who chooses the easy way out—choosing normal on the inside, but making sure you look odd to everyone else.

> What makes you different makes you great—but only when it comes from a place of authenticity.

External changes may make you feel different, and even get you some odd stares, but being different for the sake of being different actually makes you like everyone else. It makes you the eminently expendable crew member, rather than the intensely invaluable starship captain. Plenty of other people are probably trying to be that same charismatic leader in the corner office who seems to easily advance up the promotion ladder. But nobody, and I mean nobody, is quite the same as who you really are—that one-of-a kind mix of your DNA, Story, and Values. Leverage your brilliance and unleash the power that is you. Learn how to present yourself to others in a way that invites them to join you in being authentic and unleashing their own brilliance.

As we've learned, you already are great. You already possess superpowers unique to you, but you can't maximize them on your own. You need other people. Here's why: on the other side of your brilliance advantage exists something you can't readily see but will compromise you if you're not careful—your brilliance *dis*advantage.

Your Brilliance Disadvantage

Few of us see ourselves realistically. Some of us see ourselves as having more strengths than struggles. We assume that we've got most of life figured out and whatever weaknesses we may have are minimized when we play to our strengths. So we lean into our "go-to" moves and forge forward confidently in every situation, thinking we can do what needs to be done—and often end up with what usually happens whenever we assume. (Hint: it involves you, me, and a donkey.)

On the other hand, some of us see ourselves in a more negative light. We know our struggles all too well, but fail to recognize our strengths. Consequently, we assume we can't do much and lack self-confidence to live out our strengths.

Both approaches miss the mark. The reality is that each of us is wired to do some things exceptionally well, and there are some things we should, for the good of everyone, never even attempt to do. We're a blend of both, strengths and struggles, brilliance and, shall we say, non-brilliance.

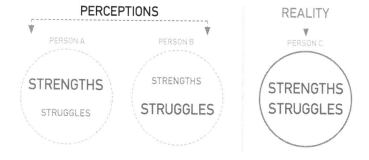

Far from limiting your effectiveness, knowing the limits of your brilliance empowers you to focus on what you do better than anyone else. And it keeps you from making some serious mistakes, frustrating those around you, and minimizing your impact.

In fact, knowing who you are can help you avoid one of the most dangerous phenomenon known to all of humanity: blind spots. A blind spot is an area of life in which people continually do not see themselves or their situation realistically. It's that lack of awareness, and sometimes complete obliviousness to reality, that causes the greatest damage.

But it's important to understand why our blind spots exist. It's not because we're defective. It's not because something went wrong in our genetic code. It's not even because we're selfish jerks, arrogant snobs, or inconsiderate losers. The very reason your blind spots exist is because you are truly exceptional at some things.

Wait. What?! Yep. That's right. Each of us has blind spots, not because we have something wrong with us, but because we have something so right that we can easily overplay our strengths in certain situations to the detriment of ourselves and others. It's not that we are defective in some way. In fact, it is because we are great in one area that we can easily miss critical perspectives in other areas.

There are some things you do that, when you bring that talent to the table or engage in a certain way, the rest of us step back in awe. We can't fathom how you do it, even though it comes so naturally. It's a strength for you, and we applaud when you step up. And yet—don't miss this—a blind spot exists on the flip side of that strength.

> A blind spot exists on the flip side of that strength.

So before you start kicking yourself again for not being perfect (remember Myth #4), know this: the only reason you have blind spots is because you have a unique mix of strengths unlike anyone else. Remember they're your "superpowers." And with great power comes great responsibility to use those strengths wisely and for the greatest good.

Think about it: The only reason Superman has superpowers is because he's from the planet Krypton. But when he forgets the source of his superpowers, when he forgets who he is and where he comes from, he exposes himself to his greatest weakness—kryptonite. And when he ignores that reality, he becomes, ironically, quite normal. Knowing his strengths allows him to define the limits of those strengths and use them wisely for the greatest good.

Now I'm not suggesting you start wearing spandex or sport a cape at the office, (that's not the weird we're looking for) but you absolutely have unique superpowers, too. However, you are not great at everything, nor should you try to be. In fact, when it comes right down to it, your greatness lies in a very narrow range. Greg McKeown, author of *Essentialism*, sums it up like this: "Only once you give yourself permission to stop trying to do it all, to stop saying yes to everyone, can you make your highest contribution towards the things that really matter." I would add that it's the fool who says, "I can do it all and better than everyone." The wise person says, "I can be me and help everyone be better."

> The fool who says, "I can do it all and better than everyone." The wise person says, "I can be me and help everyone be better."

4 Common Blind Spot Blunders

Because you are so good at certain things, you can easily overuse your brilliance in a way that puts you at a decided disadvantage or unintentionally harms other people—without your being aware of it. In other words, your natural strengths, the ones you live out when you discover who you are at the core, can position you to contribute the greatest value.

But they can also put you at a tremendous disadvantage if you're oblivious to how those strengths interact with different situations and other people who are wired differently than you. Because your natural strength behaviors feel right to you, the way others naturally see or do things can feel wrong—but it's only the result of being wired differently.

People are most comfortable in their strength zones and behave intuitively in those areas. They see farther, move faster, and respond quicker than others because of their unique wiring. However, because blind spots often occur on the flip side of our strengths, we struggle to see clearly in those areas. When we fail to see our struggles clearly, we assume we can act as if we're functioning in an area of strength when, in fact, we may be the least qualified person to deal with a situation. In those situations, we should be looking to team, not to lead. We should be stepping back, not stepping up.

Blind spots can also occur when we rely on our own natural strengths without consideration for the natural strengths and perspectives of others. For example, blind spots often become most evident when we make these 4 common blunders:

1. **We expect others to have our same strengths.** It's natural to assume everyone else can do what we do. We tend to believe this because we devalue how brilliant we are in certain areas and undervalue the brilliance of others in other areas. We often default to presuming everyone must be like us because we're comfortable with us. But no one is like us. Similar? Yes. The same? No. And even those who are similar represent only a small percentage of the population. Recognizing blind spots begins when we identify each of our diverse shades of brilliance.

2. **We see everything through the lens of our own strengths.** This one is tricky, because guess what? Each of us can only see the world through the lens of our own strengths. After all, it's who we are. However, we can minimize the risk of stumbling into a blind spot when we recognize that other valid perspectives exist. If we're smart, we'll surround ourselves with other people who see the world through different lenses and genuinely empower them to share their perspectives with us. It is not our differences that separate us. What creates distance is our unwillingness to embrace those differences to create something bigger than we could ever imagine on our own. Applied with awareness, your perspective can actually enhance another person's perspective and magnify their contribution to the world.

3. **We think our strengths are more important than the strengths of others.** This one is so easy to do. After all, you are the center of the universe aren't you? I know there are days I think so. The temptation here is to think that your own weirdness is superior to someone else's weirdness. Your brilliance is 24-karat, while theirs might only be 16-karat brilliance. Good, but not quite like yours, right?

What happens next is that you turn on your brilliance so brightly that you blind everyone else in the room. You make it quite clear that you're awesome—and everyone else leaves deflated, having never even fired up their own brilliance. Rather than having a team powered by brilliance, you're one person shining a spotlight on yourself, while everyone else scatters into the darkness. Not good, but it happens all the time. The solution is to apply your brilliance when it can do the most good, and intentionally invite others to do the same—then affirm them when they do.

Does your best sometimes cost others their best? Being the best, smartest, and brightest person in the room isn't worth much if it costs the brilliance of others. Would you prefer people to say, "You're the smartest person in the room" or "I feel so much smarter because you're in the room"?

4. **We think everyone has the same strengths we do.** John Maxwell notes, "Human nature seems to endow people with the ability to size up everybody in the world except themselves." It's easy, and even natural, to think everyone else is just like you on the inside. But that thinking comes from the worst blind spot of all: thinking you don't have blind spots. Not everyone thinks like you. Not everyone shares your life experiences. Not everyone shares your values. As a result, we don't always "get" them and, more importantly, they often don't "get" us.

The Intention—Perception Gap

When we fail to recognize the potential for blind spots, we miss the most obvious, yet often ignored reality: *Our actions are not always perceived by others in the way we intend them.* Why? Because they are not you! Each person brings their own brand of weird to every conversation. In a room full of weird people, all sorts of strange perceptions take place, likely without anyone realizing it.

The very strengths that make us great can also create struggles and friction with others, especially when we use our brilliance without considering how it might be interpreted by others. For example:

Intention: Conduct an efficient meeting.
Perception: "You don't care how I feel."

Intention: Create a high-energy work environment.
Perception: "Don't you care that I am overwhelmed?"

Intention: Seek consensus from all stakeholders.
Perception: "Why can't you just make a decision?"

Intention: Seize an opportunity to expand.
Perception: "You're making decisions too hastily."

Intention: Put better policies in writing.
Perception: "I guess it's time to update my resume."

Intention: Keep better track of employee efforts.
Perception: "Why are you such a micromanager?"

Intention: Let people take ownership of the process.
Perception: "I don't get any direction from my boss."

Intention: Train people to learn from mistakes.
Perception: "Why is she being so critical of my work?"

Intention: Offer lunch and learn opportunities.
Perception: "I never get a break and am chained to my desk."

Intention: Clear delineation of roles.
Perception: "Why are you painting me into a corner?"

Intention: Speak directly so there's no confusion.
Perception: "You're brutal and insensitive."

We don't have to try to create this gap. It happens automatically unless we're intentional about minimizing it. You naturally think like you think. You naturally lean into your own DNA hardwiring, Story, and Values. You are weird. So is everyone else. No wonder it's so challenging to communicate!

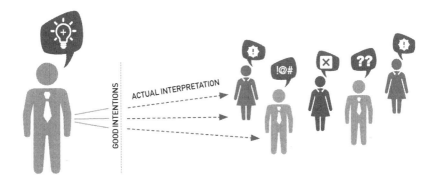

Simply recognizing the gap exists is half the battle, though. Only then can you see what was once in your blind spot before. Only then can you can identify and neutralize those places where you are experiencing the Intention-Perception Gap.

It begins with understanding how you are wired and realizing that everyone else is wired differently. It continues by getting to know what makes other people tick—on your team, in your family, or in your organizational leadership.

You need to intentionally discover what makes each of them weird as they assess and share their own Big 3—DNA, Story, and Values. Only then you can begin to consciously close the gap between intention and perception.

When you do, you position yourself and those around you to multiply your combined brilliance and create a high-performance culture people love. We'll delve deeper into how to build that culture in Step 3, but it begins right here when you start closing the gap between intention and perception by minimizing the impact of your blind spots.

The truth is our differences can empower us because everyone has a unique place where they can make the best contribution. That's what being weird is all about. It's not about trying to change you. It's not about getting other people to do what you want. It's not even about trying to change the world.

You can't change people. You can't even change most circumstances or the world around you. However, you can live authentically and embrace your weirdness. And when you do, the world around you is changed *because of you.*

The impact is extraordinary. And it all begins when one person authentically connects with another.

> You are weird. So is everyone else.
> No wonder it's so challenging to communicate!

Chapter 11

Your Authentic Path to Greater Influence

> "In our work and in our living, we must realize that difference is a reason for celebration and growth, rather than a reason for destruction." — Audre Lorde

When Al Bennett got called into an office by one of his team leaders, he wasn't quite sure what to expect. Al had been a change consultant for about four years for a large financial advisory group. But he'd be the first to tell you he's not a numbers guy. His brilliance lies in helping family businesses, especially in the farming industry, navigate generational change. But his path wasn't always so clear.

Everything shifted for him that day he sat down in the office. As all of us would when called into the boss's office, Al hurriedly ran a quick diagnostic in his head, wondering if he had somehow messed up or neglected some critical task. He thought he had enough grey hairs by that stage of his career to be credible as a consultant and had heard nothing negative about his performance.

Al's puzzled look turned to surprise when his team leader got frank with him:

Al, if you're expecting someone above you to tell you what you're going to be when you grow up, you're going to have a long wait.

That's not our culture. That's not who we are. Instead, I want you to create your own job description. I want you to create a vision for your own success. Document it, bring it back to me, and let me promote it up the chain.

As Al processed the request, he realized his team leader had just handed him an invitation—an invitation to authenticity. His authentic leader, who was committed to living out the company culture of authenticity, had invited Al to discover who he really was. He offered Al the chance to discover how best to position himself to deliver his greatest value for the organization while doing something he found personally fulfilling.

Wow! As anyone who's been in corporate America knows… that's *weird*.

Al responded to the authentic offer by surveying his personality and hardwiring (DNA), his life experiences (Story), and what really mattered to him in life (Values). As he did so, he began to see a pattern, a weird convergence of brilliance.

By nature, Al was skilled at the "soft skills" of interpersonal relationships. He excelled at connecting deeply with people, mediating and resolving conflicts, and helping other people see highly emotional situations more clearly. The farm connection had always been strong for Al because of his life experiences. Al had grown up on a farm himself, working alongside his own father, managing 1,100 acres in the late 1970s.

As he became more involved in the family business into the early 1990s, Al assumed a more prominent role in the local community and served on the County Board. He soon discovered a knack for politics and developed the know-how of working with government agencies in the highly regulated farming industry. Plus, he found he was often asked to mediate conflicts, something he enjoyed and greatly valued being able to do.

As word got out about Al's unique bend of brilliance in the late

'90s, he was asked to consult across the nation wherever conflict needed to be resolved involving farming and government service. But as he reached the end of 2000, he was forced to navigate what looked like a significant setback.

His own family farming operation relied heavily on rented land, a common practice in today's industry. However, when three of the land owners passed away, their estates were sold by the families—and Al lost the use of the land. He was forced to liquidate the family business and find a new line of work. Al felt all the emotions most people would feel then—as he describes it, "It was very frightening. I was thinking, Well if I can't farm—which is what I've been doing for 23 years—what am I going to do? Who am I going to be? I literally had to recreate myself."[25]

And that is what led him to the financial company in the first place. But now, as he intentionally responded to the invitation to greater authenticity, he got the clarity he needed. After taking a good hard look in the mirror, Al realized he really wanted to work with farm families across the United States to improve their operations and prepare them for generational change, a process often rife with interpersonal conflict and government red-tape. Al chose to build on his communication strengths and his passion for helping them create a vision, mission, and core values. To Al, it was the perfect fit for *who* he was, *why* he did it, and it aligned with *how* he wanted to go about doing *what* he did best.

The financial company loved his plan. The team leader accepted Al's proposal and championed his role in the company. As a direct result of Al living out who he was over the next several years and his modified job description, his team secured over $120 million in loan volume from a major client! The company won. Al won. And all the customers helped by Al over the years also won in a big way, both financially and emotionally. Families that otherwise would have fallen into generations of bitterness and pain instead enjoyed peaceful paths forward.

That's what authenticity does. It positions everyone to win, often in unanticipated ways, and to capitalize on opportunities for synergy that might otherwise have gone unnoticed.

Not only did Al go out and do the work, he talked about what he did. He soon became known as "the guy to call" when farming families need to navigate growth and change.

Al's role thrived until the company recently decided, through no fault of Al's, to eliminate consulting entirely from its business model. Once again, authenticity carried the day. When Al got word of the consulting phase-out, he was offered another position in the company. However, he realized trying to fit the new role would mean squeezing into someone else's Success Box. This time around, he knew how successful he could be by living out who he is. Instead, he chose to walk away from the "safe, secure job with benefits" so he could keep delivering his very best to the world in his own weird way.

It all started when one person committed to being authentic, and invited another person to do the same.

Authenticity Invites Authenticity

Think about it: we like to celebrate different and unique. We admire those who have the courage to be weird. Yet, in our own lives, we work hard to fit in and to suppress our own weirdness. All too often, we abandon our true greatness when we allow what others think, or what we *think* they think, to become the standards we live by. We think we can change things by morphing into what the world needs.

When we make the mistake of thinking we can change things in the world to unfold the way we want them to—a.k.a. manipulate reality—we only set ourselves up for slowly chipping away at our authenticity until we become a shadow of who we were designed to be. We are no longer tapping into our greatness. We are swimming against our own current.

The great influencers of the world, from Winston Churchill to Dr. Martin Luther King, from Mother Teresa to Nelson Mandela, and all the others you can recall, serve as proof that you don't change the world; the world is inspired to change because of you being you. It's the power of you being you, living out who you are with authenticity that moves other people to respond. Not only do you perform better, but other people respond to your authenticity.

Where would his country be today if Nelson Mandela had listened to his people once he became president? They wanted revenge; he wanted healing. Nelson Mandela might have fallen into the trap many of us do. He could've thought, now that I am president, I must do what a president does and submit to the wishes of the people. Instead, he lived out who he was as a man who happened to be president.

His weirdness came from his natural hardwiring (DNA) of being accommodating and understanding. His life experiences (Story) of imprisonment molded him into a man that had the discipline and courage to do what was right instead of what satisfied the environment around him. And his Values of peace, forgiveness, and unity—values shaped by both his DNA and Story—served as filters on his decision-making process that shaped the destiny of millions.

Remember the story I shared in Chapter 4 about entrepreneur Sam Riley? This talented leader I advise, has built an amazing company by embracing his weirdness as the mad scientist who generated an idea-a-minute and always challenging the status quo. He's one of the brightest, most inspiring people I've ever had the privilege to come alongside. But he lost himself when he abandoned authenticity—to the point where he seriously considered leaving all he had worked for to find his true self once again. He thought he knew what the growing organization needed him to be and what others expected him to be. But no matter how hard he tried to fit into The Success Box, it didn't work. Not only did he not get acceptance and respect, he became defeated, burned out, and frustrated.

The people of South Africa were inspired to change by the weirdness that was Nelson Mandela. An entire industry may very well be inspired to change by the weirdness of Sam.

When we're intentional about engaging other people with authenticity, we live out who we are. Who we are gives us clarity about our why. Our who and why naturally shape how we go about what we do. Great leaders don't start with why. Why is important, don't get me wrong. But the *why* that flows from a deep understanding of *who* has proven to be an unstoppable force in the history of humanity.

> The why that flows from a deep understanding of who has proven to be an unstoppable force in the history of humanity.

Start with Who

That's not to say that when you set out to live with authenticity that everything will go as smoothly as it did with Al. Not everyone will get it. Not everyone will appreciate who you really are. In fact, some people may reject who you really are. Award-winning author of *The Love Mindset* and *The Art of Talking to Yourself,* Vironika Tugaleva puts it this way:

> Self-discovery changes everything, including your relationships with people. When you find your authentic self, those who loved your mask are disappointed. You may end up alone, but you don't need to stay alone. While it's painful to

sever old connections, it's not a tragedy. It's an opportunity. Now, you can find people who understand the importance of looking for truth and being authentic. Now, you can find people who want to connect deeply, like you've always wanted to, instead of constant small talk and head games. Now, you can have real intimacy. Now, you can find your tribe.[26]

Isn't that what you really want? To connect deeply with people who resonate with and accept who you really are? We know people are naturally drawn to authenticity. The acceptance we so desperately seek only comes when we stop pursuing it. It's the simple secret every significant contributor understands. Not easy, but simple.

It starts with one person—you—choosing to be authentic in relationship with another person—one-to-one. It's about you learning how to position yourself to the world in such a way that others are invited to do the same.

Throughout our journey together in these pages, you've learned a lot about discovering who you really are. Along the way, you may have picked up on a relatively simple framework you can use to reposition your authentic self in one-to-one relationship with others.

Who → Why → How → What

Most people, and organizations, lead by telling other people *what* they do, as if their identity is defined by their occupation or activity. But as we've seen, there is far more to you than what you do. Some people get closer to the truth and think you should start with *why,* but like Benjamin Gates and the glasses in *National Treasure,* there's more to it.

If it is to be authentic, and the only way to become legendary is to be authentic, your *why* must come from who you are at your core. So, to have any hope of intentionally leveraging the power of you,

you can't start with why—you start with who, then let your why flow naturally. Any other approach will ultimately end up taking you off-course to one degree or another. And it won't fully invite others to follow your lead and create authenticity to go viral in your community, organization, or even the nation and the world.

This framework touches on some pretty deep questions we must all wrestle with to truly release the greatness within:

- ➲ WHO am I?
- ➲ WHY am I here?
- ➲ HOW do I fulfill my purpose?
- ➲ WHAT do I do exactly?

Those are vital questions each of us must probe to make the most of our existence. But you might want to start by using this basic framework for something simple, like crafting a memorable introduction you can use at networking or social events. Let me break it down piece by piece to demonstrate how it might work in that setting:

- ➲ **WHO**—Authenticity begins with who you are—and your name is the first step. Whenever possible, use the name you want used when speaking to you, not a formal title to be explained later. Consider what parts of your name might others struggle to understand. Turn those unusual parts into opportunities to make it more memorable. Use humor if appropriate.

- ➲ **WHY**—You'll make a more lasting impression by sharing your why to genuinely connect with the heart. Once you've discovered who you really are, you can capture the core passion behind why you get out of bed each morning. Be sincere, but keep it simple. Start with "I'm passionate about...I believe that...or I'm all about...." ALERT: Don't get preachy here. Less is more.

○ **HOW**—Build a simple bridge between why you do and what you do with how you go about living out your why. Answer the question someone might have after hearing your why: "So how do you do that?" Use phrases like "I help people to… I empower organizations to….." It's all in the punchy details. Your how is part of your own unique brilliance, so don't run from it!

○ **WHAT**—Time to get practical with the nuts and bolts of what you do. But keep it simple. Think "teaser," not "job description" here. Focus on quality nouns and verbs to tell your Story in a compact, yet powerful way. Close with something that invites additional questions and inspires conversation.

Here's how I might introduce myself to others using this simple framework:

My name is Greg Cagle, and I'm more than a little bit weird. That's because I'm passionate about helping people discover their purpose and fill the hole in the universe that only they can fill. I help people reconnect with who they are in an authentic way that punches normal in the face. I do it by empowering great people to embrace their weirdness, and maximize the brilliance within to achieve big dreams and build high-performing organizations.

Now, I'm not suggesting that being authentic is about using certain words at parties or reading a script at networking events. I'm talking about understanding yourself and being deeply committed to living out your true self in a way that invites others to understand who they are and live out their true selves when interacting with you. Here's the thing: it doesn't happen by accident. You must be intentional about each and every interaction.

Authenticity is at the heart of what it means to be weird. Remember, you are NOT normal. And neither is greatness.

When Authenticity Goes Viral: The Pixar Story

When individual leaders in an organization embrace authenticity—and commit to letting others do the same, you get an organization people love to talk about—like the one that started when Ed Catmull rejected that job offer from Disney.

Do you remember that story from earlier? Ed Catmull was the tech geek who always dreamed of working for Disney, and yet when he showed them his animated hand, they were so consumed with "trying to be Walt" that they missed the creative authenticity Walt embodied. They offered him a job as an Imagineer, designing a new attraction for Walt Disney World called Space Mountain. But Ed turned them down. He refused to squeeze into someone else's Success Box.

Instead he chose to chase his dream of making full-length, animated feature films. He didn't realize it at the time, but by having the courage to be authentic, he laid the cornerstone of a company whose name would become synonymous with authenticity, innovation, and over-the-top excellence—Pixar.

Pixar's success didn't happen overnight. Greatness never does. In fact, it took more than two decades for Pixar's weird Story to unfold. And it wasn't easy. But Pixar is an example of what is possible when people are free to deliver their authentic best.

After Disney rejected him, Ed Catmull continued his academic research to great acclaim. When he published his thesis in 1974 relating to computer graphics, he permanently secured lasting fame. He could have easily landed a cushy teaching position with tenure and been set for life. But his dream was to create full-length, computer-animated feature films.

Not long after he achieved notoriety for his groundbreaking

research, he met Alva Ray Smith. Smith had recently been let go by Xerox after pushing for more focus on computer graphics at the copier giant. *There would be no need for color,* he was told, *in the office of the future.* So, in 1977 Catmull and Smith found a billionaire patron willing to fund their rather expensive work. They needed computing power few people had the budget to fuel in those days. Working out of a garage in New York, they began assembling a team to achieve their dreams. But their patron had another Success Box in mind. He fancied himself a director. And so the team was tasked with bringing his visions to life. One small problem: he wasn't very good at it.

The team invested two years to create an animated short film called *Tubby the Tuba.* It was a technical marvel for its time—but an absolute disaster as a film. In short, their patron was not a storyteller. But in fact, neither were Catmull and Smith. You see, when Walt had lived out his genius, he worked with animation genius Ub Iwerks. Walt provided story-telling savvy and Ub provided the technical know-how to bring it to life. When Ub left Walt to strike out on his own, however, he faced the same problem—his stories fell flat. Ed Catmull had the technical expertise, but he didn't have the storytelling genius needed—nor the business savvy to bring it to life in the marketplace.

Over the course of a year, the team managed to disentangle themselves from their East Coast patron and regroup on the other side of the country where Catmull landed a job with a little company that was making big waves in filmmaking using computers—Lucasfilm. Catmull was given the freedom by George Lucas to build his own team. Within the first few months, however, Catmull realized the team had jumped out of one Success Box and into another. At the time, Lucasfilm was thought of as being on the cutting edge of technology in filmmaking. The truth was that Lucas used some simple animation in Star Wars, but he had very little interest in using computer animation at all going forward.

Once again, Catmull and friends did what they could with where they were. They needed Lucas's money, but George really wanted them to develop technology he could sell, not make animated films. However, because they didn't lose sight of the dream at the core of who they were, they managed to keep moving forward. They forged new ground using computer animation in *Star Trek 2: The Wrath of Khan,* for example, even though they lived under constant fear that at any moment Lucas might break up the band and send them all packing.

And that was when they first met a young guy who had recently been fired by Disney. Here was another person who'd grown up dreaming of working at Disney. Trying to avoid looking uncool, he had snuck into the 49-cent showing of *The Sword in the Stone* as a teenager. He love animated films because of—you guessed it—his passion for *storytelling.*

After graduating from Walt Disney's own "brainchild," the California Institute of the Arts, John Lasseter was hired at Disney in 1979. But like Catmull before him, John quickly realized that Walt's genius was missing—and no one seemed to notice.

John soon got the attention of everyone there, honing his craft with some of Disney's best and brightest. It was when John saw early footage of the film Tron, that he first glimpsed what was possible by uniting animation with computer graphics. "This is what Walt was waiting for," he realized. So, he pitched an idea for a computer-animated film—and got fired for it. Note this: like Catmull, Lasseter knew his idea would meet resistance. He could have kept quiet and squeezed into the Disney Success Box. But, like Catmull, he chose to remain true to who he was. He chose to be weird.

When Lasseter first joined the team at Lucasfilm, they had to disguise him as an "interface designer," because Lucas had no need for a storyteller on his "tech team." At a time when a lot of traditional animators we afraid computers would replace them, Lasseter leaned into his new gig, uniting all he knew about animation and storytelling with Catmull's technical genius.

Working nearly around the clock, Lasseter led the effort to produce an animated short called "Andrew and Wall B." At its first showing, the crowd recognized it immediately for the breakthrough it truly was. They erupted with a standing ovation even before it was over. But George Lucas thought it was awful and later said it reinforced his belief that there was no future in computer-animated films. He redoubled his efforts to get the team to create the Pixar Image Computer, a product that could be sold for high-end graphics applications.

In an ironic twist, it was this Pixar imaging computer, which no one on the team actually used to do computer animation, that first caught the attention of an entrepreneur who suddenly found himself with time on his hands.

After his first venture took off and did exceptionally well, this trail-blazing firebrand brought in a veteran from another industry to help him run things. But the guy he brought in, John Scully from Pepsi, soon ran him off. And with that, Steve Jobs found himself looking for the next big thing.

Lucas first offered to unload his Pixar imaging computer company for $50 million. Jobs waited him out and scooped up the group for only $5 million, plus a commitment to invest another $5 million in capital.

Meanwhile, back at Disney, Michael Eisner had recently taken over and planned to shut down animation all together. However, in an effort to appease Roy Disney, Walt's nephew, Eisner let Roy take over animation, thinking he was solving two problems at once. But when Roy saw the power of computer animation, he recognized the potential at once. Of everyone at Disney, Roy was the most connected to Walt's own storytelling genius. He shared the passion that had fueled Walt and his own father. His awareness of his own Story moved him to see what others could not. So, the door was creaking open for working with Disney yet again.

Nevertheless, Catmull and Lasseter had not arrived, not by a long shot. Steve Jobs had yet another Success Box to cram them in. Jobs' interest wasn't in making feature films or telling stories. Not at all. His interest was in "tiny little machines." In keeping with his mission at Apple, he wanted to disrupt the status quo and make graphics capability available to everyone. In short, he wanted a product he could sell. At first he thought he had it in the Pixar Image Computer.

Fortunately for the team, Jobs was busy trying to launch another venture, his NeXT computer company. So, once again, the team continued to follow their dreams "on the side," cramming computer-animated film work in whenever they could. It was during these cram sessions that Lassetter began blending storytelling with an element that had been a trademark of Walt's own animation efforts—humor. His first test subject? A "baby" Luxo lamp called Luxo Jr.

For the first time, the team began exploring whether or not inanimate objects could have dramatic value as they showed the little lamp playing alongside its protective "parent lamp." The answer after their first test showing? Yes. John knew they were on to something when the first question he got after the showing was not about the technical expertise involved in the making of the film, but, "Was the parent lamp the mom or the dad?"

Because of the authentic culture on the team, Catmull's technical expertise was seamlessly integrating with Lasseter's storytelling savvy more every day. The results looked promising. But Jobs didn't see it. Year after year he continued to pour millions into the venture. After it became evident that the Pixar computer wasn't a winner, Jobs claimed it had never been about the hardware, but software, and announced to the world that the rendering software that the team had developed had been his primary focus all along. One former employee who had been brought in to build technology even stated:

"It's clear they wanted to make movies and were only pretending to be a computer company."

As Disney used the Pixar software and saw more of the genius emerging from Lasseter's animation efforts, they offered him a job as a film director for big money. But John turned them down, saying, "I can go to Disney and be a director, or I can stay here and make history." But in 1988, Steve Jobs, business genius, didn't believe Pixar could make movies. So he started them making commercials to generate revenue. Once again, the team sucked it up and worked in their real passion alongside.

Finally in 1990, Jobs sold off the computer hardware business. He was running out of patience. In 1990 alone the company took an $8.93 million loss. The blow-ups between Jobs and other team member became so severe that Alva Ray Smith left the company, physically ill from his interactions with Jobs. Then Jobs made a shrewd business move that nearly killed the culture. In an effort to get back at least some of the almost $50 million he had poured into the business, he took back everyone's equity in the company. In the face of financial failure, Steve Jobs leaned into who he was. For better or worse, and regardless of how many people liked him at the end of the day, he refused to accept defeat. Jobs still had a significant role to play, one that could only be filled by someone with his unique brilliance.

Fortunately, the company had a good deal of momentum by then in its dealing with Disney. Catmull and Lassetter sensed they were close to the breakthrough they'd always dreamed of. Jobs had found a way to get a deal done with Disney to license part of the Pixar imaging software. Now he negotiated with Disney to make the first computer-animated feature film, *Toy Story,* and ensured that Pixar would get full credit for its role.

In classic Jobs fashion, when the Toy Story deal was announced, Steve claimed that making films had always been his goal at Pixar. Of course, Catmull and Lassetter agreed. Yet just a few months prior to the release of *Toy Story*, Jobs was still trying to unload Pixar to Microsoft. Clearly the drivers of the Pixar culture, Catmull and Lasseter were the ones who understood and fueled the unique Pixar culture. But they still needed to let Jobs be Jobs.

What the mercurial entrepreneur finally realized was that he didn't have a product to sell, nor did he have software to sell. But he did have a company to sell. And once *Toy Story* released to acclaim, Jobs wagered there would be a lot of people who would want to own a piece of Pixar.

So Jobs made plans to take the company public just one week after the Thanksgiving release of *Toy Story*. He brought in experienced execs to appease Wall Street. As a result, Ed Catmull was demoted, but, get this—Ed was fine with it! Why? His dream wasn't to run a company, remember. It was to make computer-animated feature films. That was his Story, and he was sticking to it.

Just a few days after Toy Story made box-office history, Jobs made a little history of his own. On the first day of the IPO for Pixar, Jobs made over $1.1 billion. And Catmull, Lasseter, and the Pixar team were on their way to redefining the filmmaking industry and the future of animation.

It only happened because a handful of people remained true to who they really were—in all their unique brilliance—and invited others to do the same. In doing so, they created an authentic culture that sustained them through nearly twenty years of distractions. It energized them to work around the clock and to push past impossible barriers to achieve the goal. Now that's not to say everyone always went about living out their weirdness in the best way, but had each of them not been free do what he did best, the world would never have known the joy brought to it by Pixar.

And don't forget, just a few years after the release of *Toy Story*, it was Disney that was begging to partner with Pixar, not the other way around.

If there is one thing we can learn from this story, it is to be fearless in the pursuit of what sets your soul on fire. That's the power of authenticity. And when it goes viral in an organization's culture—look out! Greatness isn't far behind.

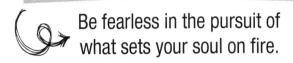

Be fearless in the pursuit of what sets your soul on fire.

Chapter 12

The Secret Fuel for High-Performing Cultures

"The real competitive advantage in any business is one word only—people." — Kamil Toume

For a few years now I have been working with a company that not only understands the value of maximizing how people are wired for success, but has also built a business model around cultivating authenticity in children at a very early age.

It all started in 1972 in the back of a family home in Auckland, New Zealand. As a primary school teacher, Glennie was one day researching occupations which she could engage in while still having her children with her and thought, *If I can handle 42 children in a class-room, I should be able to care for a similar group of pre-schoolers with extra help.* She looked at her own hard-wiring and education background—plus the need to make a living as a mom—and stepped out to start the new venture with only $800 to her name.

The journey wasn't easy. She met resistance at every turn, especially because education in New Zealand is generally publicly owned and heavily regulated. Becoming a single mom four years later added to her challenges. During the 1980s, it took a lot of wrangling to get officials to recognize private education. But she persisted to form what eventually became Kindercare Learning Centres in New Zealand. As more women entered the workforce during the 1990s, demand for their unique services skyrocketed.

In their 45th year in 2017, Kindercare opened its 45th location! By all accounts, Kindercare has become one of New Zealand's most reliable and unique private education services. What started in the back of a family home 45 years ago has become a successful and revolutionary early childhood care and education model—because what they do is unlike anything I've seen done in education. In fact, you could say it's weird.

Touring their facilities, I was blown away by what I saw—a calm, enriching environment where every child was positioned to let his or her unique brilliance shine. I saw an intentional plan to provide all types of environments to meet a child's natural preferences. Children were allowed to naturally navigate to whatever learning station most interested them. Even though the children were very young, the environment was noticeably calm and orderly. None of the children were anxious or rambunctious, because each was empowered to satisfy his or her curiosity through whatever appealed to their natural tendencies.

What makes Kindercare so special is their focus on the individual child. They know that each child is unique and possesses their own set of gifts and talents. They recognize those gifts and nurture them as the child grows, developing their natural abilities and inclinations at a young age. Helping each child reach their full potential through loving connections and respectful care is at the forefront of their mission. They know that children, like adults, don't belong in a one-size-fits-all box, hence their holistic, play-based approach to learning. They value physical health in addition to mental stimulation. They offer a nutritional program designed to give children the energy to perform at their best. They invest a large part of the day helping each child establish beneficial rituals that will maximize their natural talents. And by partnering closely with parents, they are able to improve successful outcomes for each child by aligning what they do with the child's natural rhythms of life at home.

You may be thinking, How could they possibly know a child's hardwiring at such an early age? Here's where it really gets weird. Through their Excel Education Program, they carefully observe and identify each child's interests, so they can create a customized development plan. They base their program on solid research that reveals the connection between a child's emotional development and educational development. They recognize that unless children have a strong emotional competence platform (EQ), they will not learn (IQ) or adapt (LifeQ) to others as quickly as they otherwise would.

Through their "You Can Do It" program, they support each child's confidence, persistence, and resilience. They encourage the children to self-manage and not to break down when things don't go their way. But their commitment to fostering greater authenticity doesn't end there. They created the Living and Learning Foundation, a Trust to provide high-quality care for children from struggling socioeconomic backgrounds, maximizing the brilliance of those whose stories might otherwise have held them back.

All of this stemmed from the dream of one woman who chose to be her authentic self. She chose to be weird—and built a company committed to helping children to discover who they are and how to live out their authenticity from an early age.

Now with Glennie's son Kelly at the helm, Kindercare continues to empower children to live with authenticity so they can deliver their very best to the world. It's amazing! And it's exactly the formula organizations must follow to create high-performance cultures that deliver over-the-top results consistently. [28]

Hey, Leaders, Authenticity Starts with You!

There is great power in staying true to who we are and living that out in an authentic way, but that power gets multiplied exponentially when we allow others to do the same thing. It must begin one-to-one, as we discovered in the previous chapter, with each person choosing to engage and be engaged with authenticity. That takes effort. And it's not a one-time thing. Every day, every meeting, every interaction must be undergirded by this commitment to be weird. After all, normal gets us disengaged employees and the high costs that go with it.

A Gallup poll discovered that disengagement in the workplace costs more than just those minutes of Facebook scrolling. US industry loses between $450-550 *billion* each year in productivity damage.[29] In addition, the consequences of a nearly 70% disengaged workforce show up in stifled communication between employees and upper administration, stagnated creativity, and startling turnover costs—estimated to be a whopping 100%-300% of the replaced employees' base salaries. Employers think that they are losing their people to higher paying jobs. Instead, they are losing them because their people feel unacknowledged, unencouraged, and boxed in by their work culture.[30]

Think about it. If you're doing what you are wired to do, and you love to do it because it aligns with your Story and values, wouldn't you be excited about going to work every day? I contend that the reason so many employees are disengaged today is that they are not working in a culture that encourages them to discover and live out who they really are in a way that maximizes value for the entire team and organization.

But here's the good news. That problem can be solved. I've already showed you the essentials required for someone to discover who they really are and to begin to live that out one-to-one. And that is key, because leaders define and shape culture. Dr. Henry Cloud, author of *Boundaries for Leaders* puts it this way: "Culture is shaped by what leaders create and allow."[31] It's both active and passive. You see, it all comes back to leadership. And that influence can be good or bad, depending on the leader.

I've worked with highly-skilled people who try to lead others the way they themselves like to be led. They work towards the desired outcome by doing it their way and want others to go about it the same way they do. Remember the myth from earlier: "There's only one way to do it"? Rather than creating a culture in which other people could lead based on who they are, they created that Success Box we met earlier and expected everyone to squeeze into it.

> "Culture is shaped by what leaders create and allow."
> — Dr. Henry Cloud

So an authentic culture begins with an authentic leader—every time. Without leaders committed to living out who they are with authenticity, you can forget about an authentic culture. It can't happen. Not *won't*, but *can't*.

Remember the *Harvard Business Review* study I mentioned way back when we started this weird journey together? Researchers interviewed 125 highly successful leaders to see what they did that led to their success. They were hoping to discover some secret sauce they could bottle and share with the rest of us. They engaged these leaders across a wide range of ages, industries, races, religions, and socio-economic backgrounds. They analyzed more than 3,000 pages of transcripts from extensive interviews to find what made these leaders effective.

And they discovered [gasp!] "that being authentic made them more effective." Those leaders who were in tune with who they are— their Big 3: DNA, Stories, and Values—proved to be the best at getting high-performance results. Their self-awareness unlocked their unique brilliance.

Leaders who succeed take the time to figure *themselves* out first. They identify their own strengths, weaknesses, and behavioral tendencies. They become students of their own Story. They choose their values carefully. And let's be clear about one thing: all of us have the spark of leadership in us, because we all influence someone.

So, if you as a leader are not committed to greater self-awareness and tapping into what makes you great, you can forget about building a great organization. Even if you do manage to put the pieces together in the right way and all the stars briefly align in the business heavens, it won't be sustainable. You'll default to squeezing everyone into a success box that looks an awful lot like you.

> **Leaders who succeed take the time to figure themselves out first.**

Eventually this pressure to conform creates an inauthentic culture of sameness rather than one defined by vibrant authenticity. An inauthentic culture creates a group of compliant people who carry out the wishes of their managers and leaders. It can be efficient, scalable, and sometimes very productive. It can also be successful for some time until it gets left in the dust when some other organization disrupts the status quo. Think Blockbuster and Netflix, Blackberry and Apple, Yahoo and Google, or any brick-and-mortar retailer and Amazon.

Are you unknowingly creating—because of your own inauthenticity—an inauthentic culture that holds your team back? If you don't know who YOU are as a leader in your organization, how authentic is your influence on those around you? Authenticity invites authenticity. Who you are as a leader will determine the performance of your team culture. The first step to creating an authentic culture within your organization is to create an environment that champions the authenticity of its people.

7 Questions to Ask for Greater Self-Awareness

One of the biggest issues I run into when coaching and training leaders is a glaring lack of self-awareness. In some ways, I get it. As we noted earlier, the ironic part of knowing your strengths is that you often don't realize they are strengths because they come so easily to you. This reality can create a blind spot on the back side of your strength when you overuse it. Often, it's only when I come along and ask probing questions that force self-examination that leaders begin to develop greater self-awareness.

Here's a "hot list" of questions to self-diagnose your own level of self-awareness. These are questions anyone wanting to build an authentic culture *must* answer:

1. **Are you squeezing into someone else's Success Box?** This is an easy trap to fall into, because once you begin to conform to others' expectations and are rewarded, it becomes a very enticing shortcut to pursue. But in the long run it erodes who you are, minimizes your contribution, and eventually renders you ineffective.

2. **Have you identified your most dangerous blind spots?** Your natural strengths can position you to contribute the greatest value to your team. But they can also create something we all have— blind spots. Blind spots reside on the flip side of our strengths, which is why we struggle to see them clearly. When you rely on your strengths too heavily and overuse them, you compromise your advantage in that situation. You alienate others by creating a perception that does not align with your intention. In some cases, you may overuse your strengths so much that you completely lose your advantage and become disadvantaged. This effect is most likely to occur under stress or tight time constraints.

3. **How well do you interact with people who are your personality opposites?** We struggle to understand the perspective of people who are wired differently than we are. Consequently, two people whose strengths are at opposite ends of a personality factor have a greater chance for disconnect. It takes intentional understanding and greater awareness to bridge that gap.

4. **What are the relationship keys that will position you to take your leadership to the next level?** By figuring out how best you relate to others, you can head off potential problems before they develop. Understanding your natural inclinations alerts you to potential challenges when trying to connect with people and move from authoritative to permissive.

5. **How are you naturally wired to deal with confrontation?** Conflict is unavoidable. It's part of the human condition. There are people that engage in conflict, want to resolve conflict, want to avoid conflict, or want to restrict conflict. Knowing your natural tendencies allows you to be effective in dealing with conflict. The question is: do you care enough about others to discover how you are wired to deal with it? By understanding your natural response to conflict, you can leverage your strengths and avoid creating additional struggles for everyone. If you don't know how you are wired, you may be unaware of the impact you are having—regardless of your intention. If you understand how you are naturally wired for confrontation, you can choose your best response to situations that could potentially produce conflict.

6. **Do you know your natural response to change and why it matters for the health of your team?** We live in a world of rapid change. If you don't like change, you'll like irrelevance even less. For a

leader to succeed, he or she must be out in front to encourage change and growth and show how to make it happen. But that doesn't mean everyone is naturally wired to embrace change. In fact, every person is wired to respond to change differently. Your hard-wired response to change is neither good nor bad in itself. But knowing it prepares you to seize change as an opportunity.

7. **Are you leveraging your behavioral hard-wiring to increase influence?** Understanding how you are wired to lead and succeed empowers you to lift your leadership lid. When you know your own strengths and struggles, you can better set priorities for growth and identify situations where you can deliver maximum value to others. Your ability to influence others—for better or worse—always determines your effectiveness and your potential for success. Personal success without influence brings only limited effectiveness. Greatness requires intentional effort on your part.

Only when you dig deep to uncover the answers can you empower your team to do the same and unleash the power of authenticity throughout your culture. An organization is nothing more than a group of individuals coming together for a common purpose or goal. The individual is where the magic lies. When leaders stay true to their own authenticity and allow those around them to be authentic as well, then the organization is on its way to being truly great and defined by execution excellence.

The Same Old, Same Old Sameness

A dynamic, authentic place is not where most people live today. They live in a world of sameness. High-quality sameness, but highly expendable sameness nonetheless. Our surplus society has a surplus of similar companies employing similar people with similar educational backgrounds coming up with similar ideas producing similar things with similar prices and similar quality. This reality has created what Tom Peters calls the 10X Phenomenon—10 times better, but 10 times less different.[32] That's why having an authentic culture gives an organization a tremendous competitive advantage.

There is a huge and quantifiable difference between inauthentic culture and authentic culture. One drives people to compliance at best and departure at worst. The other raises the level of commitment and inspires people to be proactive thinkers and problem solvers.

One creates a mind numbing, uninspired sleep-walk through predetermined actions.

The other creates a vision that begs to be followed and activates creativity, innovation and risk taking.

One assumes that brilliance and cutting-edge contribution is predictable and controllable. The other knows that healthy dissatisfaction with the status quo, healthy debate—that produces what's right instead of being right—and brilliant ideas are not predictable.

Innovative ideas can't spawn from the primordial soup of conformity. Brilliance doesn't always reveal itself in a neatly organized way. Like life itself, it can be sloppy, disorganized, sometimes frustrating—but always exciting and satisfying.

And the most important thing: authentic cultures always start with WHO. They begin with weird. One weird leader lives out his or her unique brilliance, then empowers another to do the same, and another, until an entire weird culture is driving their every move. Why? An organization is a living, dynamic thing, just like an individual person. And like any member of the Be Weird clan, organizations powered by authentic cultures shape their own destinies, rather than waiting for the next Amazon to knock them off.

> **Authentic cultures always start with WHO.**

In today's business environment, if a company wants to be an industry leader, have a dynamic high-performance culture, and grow year after year, it has to become Over-the-Top in everything it does.

Over-The-Top [Adjective]: Far more than usual or expected; based on a mixture of desire and boldness. Antonym: *Average*. Ugh.

Companies have to rethink their strategy and reinvent their business models on a regular basis. Execution has to be strategically driven, tactically managed, value-metric focused, continuously improving with no point of failure. Then once you've gotten there, you have to sustain that level of performance. And the only way that gets done is if authentic leaders intentionally create the authentic cultures that produce Over-The-Top results.

Authentic Cultures Deliver
Over-the-Top Results

It's been said that the solutions we seek lie in the quality of our questions. So, I have a question for you: How often do you hear these types of questions being asked in your organization, department, or team?

- ➲ Can we do things differently?
- ➲ What do you need from me?
- ➲ How can we avoid this problem in the future?
- ➲ What's the best way for me to help the team?
- ➲ How can our departments better work together?
- ➲ How might we work together to speed things up?
- ➲ What if we did it this way?
- ➲ Are there improvements we can make to exceed our customers' expectations?

Questions like these are generated by authentic people in authentic cultures. When employees are asking these types of questions, the organization is on its way to achieving great things with high-performing individuals driving initiatives forward, embracing opportunities to initiate change, and taking personal responsibility for their contribution to the organization. They have no problem being held accountable to the organization and to their fellow employees. They aren't afraid of debate nor conflict and understand the value in both achieving effective change as well as innovation.

It's questions like these that lead to statements like:

- ➲ I have an idea.
- ➲ I'll take responsibility for that.
- ➲ I'd like to work on this solution.
- ➲ Let's discuss this with everyone on the team.
- ➲ I like our improvement. With a little more teamwork, I think we can improve more.
- ➲ I'd like to spend some time sharing with you what I've learned here.
- ➲ I need your help, because I want to make sure this meets expectations.

Everyone wants to be a part of a high-performance organization that's thriving, innovative, and growing with a long, bright future. To have that type of organization, there must be thriving, innovative, growing *individuals* with long and bright futures so the company isn't doomed to a mediocre existence or, even worse, a slow painful death.

So how do we create that? It's simple, right? Change the way people think and act, the way they react to problems, the way they work together, innovate, and become solution-oriented thinkers, and you change them into "Change Makers." Once you've done that, you've transformed the company—at least, that's how many leaders think. This thinking is demonstrated in their training programs, employee reviews, and company policies.

The authentic leader thinks differently. He or she realizes that changing people doesn't produce great companies. Helping people discover what makes them brilliant and then allowing them to live that out in vivid 4K color is the secret—then carefully placing people together where their strengths are magnified and their weakness is made irrelevant.

Authentic cultures occur when leaders don't try to tell people what to think. They create an environment that encourages people to think—and each to think in his or her uniquely brilliant way.

Now don't get me wrong here; I know there are certain things that have to be done certain ways. Leaders are required to teach people a very specific way of doing certain things, the same way every time. I'm not talking about skills. I'm talking about things like problem-solving, collaboration, relationship-building, and other similar competencies that are critical to organizational success.

The key is allowing the analyzer to analyze, the challenger to challenge, the director to direct, the abstract innovator to innovate, and everyone to do what they do best. And the entire time they are doing what they do best, they respect and embrace the differences of those around them, resulting in a broader perspective.

How does an organization achieve this? It begins with leaders who have the courage to embrace their individuality and dare to be weird.

They have to be willing to…

- ➲ Be vulnerable and share their weakness with their team.
- ➲ Ask questions rather than bark out statements.
- ➲ Listen with the intent to understand an opposing viewpoint, rather than listening with the intent to reply.
- ➲ Say things like "I don't know. What do you think?" "I'm sorry. I made a mistake." and "I need your help."

Authentic leaders intentionally work on understanding their value and knowing when the circumstances put them at an advantage or a disadvantage. They understand the strengths of the people on their team and are constantly leveraging and growing those strengths. They don't expect team members to conform; they expect them to be weird and authentic—true to who they are.

Chapter 13

Weird Eats the Competition for Breakfast

Authenticity gives your organization the
character within its culture to sustain growth
and go beyond its past best performance.

Companies with weird cultures eat the competition for breakfast. But they don't do it by focusing on the competition. They achieve over-the-top results by leaning into who they truly are—and living it out together in a radically authentic way that invites others to join them.

One such company I've been privileged to work with is in Florence, Italy—La Marzocco. Not surprisingly, the CEO is one of the most authentic leaders I've ever known. As a result, he invites everyone in the company to be authentic as well, to join him in celebrating the weirdness. In fact, the La Marzocco culture demands it—and always has.

The story of La Marzocco began in 1927 when two brothers, Giuseppe and Bruno Bambi, were commissioned to create a custom espresso machine. When their sponsor turned down their final product, the two brothers chose to move forward, working out of a workshop to craft beautiful, high quality, superbly-crafted, and uniquely-designed espresso machines with great attention to detail.

It seems only fitting that the two artisans would begin in Florence, birthplace of the Italian Renaissance and home to such geniuses as Leonardo da Vinci, Michelangelo, and Brunelleschi who created some of the most celebrated works of art in the world. Their efforts would eventually result in La Marzocco becoming the industry leader in high-end coffee makers that it is today. But the road to success wasn't always easy. Authenticity never is.

At the time, the two brothers didn't have a production line. They had a passion for excellence and made every machine to order, designing each machine to fit the barista's needs and to coordinate with the decor of each location. The result of the laborious process was a hand-made, finely-tuned espresso machine that doubled as a work of art. Their attention to detail set them apart; they even made their own screws.

As a result of their authentic passion for design, La Marzocco developed and patented the first coffee machine with a horizontal boiler in 1939, now an industry standard. Although World War II brought production to a halt, the entrepreneurial spirit of the Bambi brothers led to the registration of a new patent in 1945, enabling the company to return to business as usual. The 1950s brought more innovation with lever machines using spring-activated pistons to push pressed water through the coffee, transforming the taste. In short, espresso machines became iconic, yet complex, so the focus at La Marzocco over the next several decades was on connecting with baristas, simplifying user operations while improving machine ergonomics, and producing only the highest quality machines, in spite of multiple challenges, including a flood that devastated most of Florence.

The brothers' insistence on authenticity in pursuing their craft with excellence and genuinely connecting with people guided their direction. Respect for the rich heritage of coffee—and its ability to bring people together—plus their passion in the search for quality and superior reliability are factors which have always distinguished and interested the entire company. Even today, highly specialized personnel supervise each stage in the production of every single machine, hand-crafted to order for each and every client.

When the electronic era and the automated production line changed the world of manufacturing in the 1980s, the Bambi brothers remained true to who they were. They thought the use of electronics would cheapen the product and minimize the baristas' skills that unite man and machine to produce the perfect cup of coffee. They paid a high price for their authenticity, because nearly everyone was clamoring for the much more expensive super-automatic or fully automatic" machine technology. Thanks to the use of electronics, interaction from the barista was minimized because the preparation of the beverage was almost entirely effected at the push of a button. The coffee suppliers were buying less expensive machinery from the espresso coffee machine manufacturers and putting them out on a free loan basis to their customers such as bars and coffee shops. Many suppliers even offered "free" espresso machines to cafes who signed up for a long-term coffee contract. Consequently, the market became flooded with cheaper machines. But the Bambi brothers continued to do what they thought was best for the industry and the best use of their skills.

As a result, they became the best at producing machines that consistently produced high-quality coffee. So when a growing coffee chain named Starbucks needed to ensure a similar coffee experience from one location to another, they turned to La Marzocco.

How La Marzocco got on Starbucks radar is, in itself, an example of the power of an authentic culture. At some point during the 1970s, a group of Seattle hippies who looked like they had just left Woodstock, took an interest in the craft of making fine coffee. They decided to travel to Venice and throughout the northeastern part of Italy to explore the world of coffee, but encountered nothing but doors slammed in their faces.

No doubt their hippie appearance contributed to that effect, but they decided to visit Florence and reach out to a coffee machine factory that just happened to be La Marzocco. There, the beatniks encountered something different, something weird. Rather than turning away these odd-looking foreigners, the Bambi family was delighted to share their passion for coffee-making. They spent hours teaching them the finer points of manufacturing espresso equipment, not expecting anything in return.

After this unique Seattle group went back to the States, they ordered a couple of espresso machines. They developed a relationship with a Tuscan wine dealer in Florence as well. Together, they managed to get both the wine and the La Marzocco espresso machines into some Seattle restaurants. As a direct result of this Seattle connection, when Starbucks needed consistent, high-end machines, they knew who to turn to.

When Starbucks needed to scale, these Seattle connections enabled La Marzocco, now under the leadership of second generation Piero Bambi, to build an American factory to provide the high-end machines required for Starbucks to grow. And that might have been the end of a good story right there, except that things then took a turn—which at first didn't seem to be for the better.

As Starbucks grew, it wanted to create efficiencies. And so La Marzocco had a choice: try to squeeze into the Starbucks Success Box and be known as "the ones who supply Starbucks coffee shops all over the world," or walk away from the most dominant name on the coffee business—but remain true to who they were.

La Marzocco chose to be weird. They chose to walk away.

They chose to lean into what they did best and focus on one thing, creating machines that appealed to people who loved coffee as much as they did and who embraced the rich heritage and story behind the coffee tradition. As a result of their decision to embrace authenticity, La Marzocco experienced steady growth until 2008 when the financial collapse affected them as it did the rest of the world. That trying season prompted some corporate soul-searching that moved the new managing director, Guido Bernardinelli, to intentionally cultivate the weird culture and embrace their radical commitment to authenticity—as a competitive advantage.

In a counter-intuitive move, they began developing even more expensive espresso machines that would appeal to essentially the Formula One drivers of the coffee world. Nobody had the guts to do that before in the barista world. To add to the brand's mystique, they built an entire experience around the product, because the story was too intricate to be communicated at a crowded trade show as "just another exhibit." They started their own off-site trade show experiences instead, inviting people into a garage nearby to experience the La Marzocco difference.

The response blew them away. Rather than turning off customers, they found that people were blown away by the custom experience—and loved the higher-end machines. The entire coffee world started buzzing about them. Even the press got excited. In the midst of a global recession, Guido heard customers at their shows saying, "I know that La Marzocco machine is twenty thousand bucks, but I gotta have it!" They began to feel the effects of being known for greatness.

Inspired by their initial success, Guido and the team started building an authentic community around their Story, inviting even their competitors into their learning environments. In short, they became a lifestyle company, leveraging the power of events to authentically connect people around the globe to the cause of great coffee.

To this day, every single machine is made to order in the area of Florence, Italy. Espresso machines and grinders are exported to over 100 countries with the support of branch offices in Australia, China, Germany, Korea, New Zealand, Spain, the United States, the United Kingdom, and through an international distribution network. And in each of these areas, events empower the La Marzocco team to spread their viral vision:

- ➲ *la marzocco local:* An opportunity to meet and chat all things coffee with the localized network.
- ➲ *true artisan café:* An original "pop-up", rotating-roasters coffee shop concept to promote specialty.
- ➲ *out of the box:* An event setting the example and communicating our territorial excellence to drive a change.

As they put it themselves, "We value our community and heritage and design signature events that are rich in content, dedicated to partners, industry professionals and enthusiasts from around the globe. We promote and celebrate coffee culture, bringing people together through our common passion!" As a result, they have become known as the ones who not only make the most memorable cup of coffee on the planet, but also the ones who have created a dynamic community in which coffee lovers all over the globe can thrive.

At the time of this writing, they're in the process of converting their original factory in Florence, where they manufactured espresso machines for fifty years, into a cultural center where they can share history and heritage while training about coffee, espresso machines, and leadership. *Accademia*, as it will be called, will be a center for espresso excellence, thought leadership, and research, as well as an industrial museum. It will promote academic partnerships, strategic alliances, and co-marketing initiatives while serving as a vehicle to communicate social responsibility. They've united a superior product with a fascinating story and a unique destination in Florence, Italy, steeped in coffee history to drive their reinvigorated and deeply-authentic message.

All of that is amazing, and a direct result of their tradition of choosing to be authentic. But the most amazing part of my experience with La Marzocco has been the authentic culture that powers the people within the company to do what they do.

As part of their cultural renewal after the global recession, they began having candid discussions about how to create a company environment that everyone wants to work in. As a result, they started focusing even more on people and creating a tight team culture. They began doing simple things to increase transparency and communication, like having staff meetings with the workers at all levels to share company objectives, goals, and the vision beyond basic tasks.

Forty staff people sat down together and, over the course of a year, defined the corporate mission, vision, and values. They included everyone in the success, encouraging innovation and rewarding everyone who came up with a winning idea, regardless of their job title. They encouraged each person to lean into his or her strengths and natural hardwiring. Soon the culture had gone viral, authenticity in leaders inviting great authenticity in everyone. They created a culture that I have personally experienced where people feel comfortable sharing ideas.

As a result, some of their best marketing ideas have come from people who have nothing to do with marketing. Here's how Chris Salierno, La Marzocco's Marketing Director describes the weird culture:

> We try to create a safe place where people can feel like they can contribute, and they're not intimidated to share an idea that even goes beyond what they normally do. We spend a lot of time talking about our heritage and how we got to where we are today after 90 years. We talk a lot about the people that have brought us here, those who've given us the opportunity to do what we do at the place where we work. We are very transparent with our goals. And then, we try to create a place where people can go out and do great things, and become leaders in our industry, hopefully at

La Marzocco. But I don't have many, if any, examples of people leaving our company. We have a great, loyal team of highly-motivated people that work with us. The best investment of my time as a marketer is with the people that work at our company, because they go out and amplify our message. They're the best marketers of La Marzocco that we could ever hope for.

As a result of their embracing all it means to be a weird culture, La Marzocco has seen its sales multiply in roughly a decade from about 1,600 units to over 16,000 per year. Revenue has likewise skyrocketed to 110 million euros in consolidated revenue in 2017. The future of the company is bright, as anyone who engages with them routinely encounters expressions of authenticity like these:

"Quality means doing it right when no one is looking."
—Henry Ford.

"Do not go where the path may lead, go instead where there is no path and leave a trail." — Ralph Waldo Emerson

"Actions express priorities." — Mahatma Gandhi

And my personal favorite: "The people at La Marzocco are the creators of what we have become—and what we will be."

Authenticity Changes Things

When you focus on your authenticity and allow those around you to do the same, positive disruption is bound to be the result. Consequently, when an organization begins to build a weird and authentic culture, two things happen to the makeup of the team.

First, it allows a natural departure for those that don't belong to the new reality of weird. Not everyone on your team right now will make the journey, I'm sorry to say. Yes, people will leave. But often, they will self-select to depart. If being real isn't their thing, they'll feel awkward and look for ways out on their own. You won't have to show them the door. They'll see the exit sign themselves and depart.

And that's OK. Because the people who remain and who join the new direction are the ones who will help you grow the authentic culture you desire. Your shifted focus on authenticity will inspire those who *do* belong to recommit to excellence, to innovate and solve problems, and to carry out positive change. They'll come to work with what I call *frontline obsession*—energized and engaged, eager to take the vision "out into the streets" and share it with the world. They'll charge up the hill because they know who they are, why they do what they do, and how to go about it.

Clarity produces confidence, lowers the negative stress, and motivates everyone to take one more step than they ever thought possible. That's why culture matters so much—it's at the heart of everything. No matter how good you think your strategy may be, when culture and strategy fight, culture always wins. No matter how talented you think your people may be, an inauthentic culture can cripple the best of their efforts. And in a crowded, competitive marketplace,

> When culture and strategy fight, culture always wins.

your authentic culture gives your team an invisible advantage to blow by the competition.

No two cultures are alike. That's why, when I come alongside CEOs and executive teams, I don't offer one-size-fits-all solutions. If I am going to be authentic, I've got to get to know each situation independently to discover what makes the leaders, mission, and team setting unique. I never assume I know someone's brilliance, neither for an individual nor a team.

Now, let me be clear: This doesn't happen overnight, nor is it easy. And that's what scares away most people. After all, everyone else seems to be fine with settling for normal. Why do all that extra work, right? Well, if after all this time together, you're still "in" with normal, then there's not much I can do for you. Love 'ya, but you can forget about ever achieving greatness.

And that's too bad. Because for those willing to make the journey to wyrd, an authentic culture will give your team an unprecedented competitive advantage. It can be difficult to quantify, because it is driven by critical intangibles like trust and understanding—yet it produces real-life, bottom-line, jaw-dropping results.

Here are a few things authentic cultures do that position teams to go OVER THE TOP:

Authenticity Changes Things

At the cornerstone of every authentic culture is a deep sense of trust. From the C-Suite to entry-level personnel, trust is paramount. When people understand their Big 3 and have a sense of who they are, trust accelerates within an organization and restores humanity as people engage one another with fresh vigor. A culture of trust values each individual because it knows that their uniqueness is built on their strengths.

Stephen Covey didn't exaggerate when he described the power of trust:

> Nothing is as fast as the speed of trust. Nothing is as fulfilling as a relationship of trust. Nothing is as inspiring as an offering of trust. Nothing is as profitable as the economics of trust. Nothing has more influence than a reputation of trust.

Trust is the foundation for teamwork. Authentic cultures empower teams driven by engaged members. Trust removes the barriers of fear because when employees know the organization accepts and embraces them for who they are, fear gets stripped from the equation. As confidence rises, so does productivity and innovation.

Authentic Cultures Create a Place for Teams to Flourish

Authentic cultures create a safe place to be wrong or to fail. When people feel safe, they're more willing to think creatively, take calculated risks, and try new things. Barriers to change are broken down or completely eliminated because no one fears failure.

Authenticity by nature encourages a trial-and-error approach to innovation and problem solving. Organizations that have fully authentic cultures can execute on change initiatives at 5 times the speed of other cultures.

In fact, the best companies don't want carbon copies of their employees. They want individuals who embrace their weirdness and run with it. This type of culture is the fertile ground where teams flourish and creativity blossoms. Most importantly, authentic cultures help you retain your best employees because they feel valued and safe to be who they are.

Authentic Cultures Harness Everyone's Strengths

The most authentic cultures recognize that their employees can't be good at everything. Rather than viewing this as a problem, they view it as an opportunity. You can maximize innovation by unleashing your employees to use their strengths. Think of it like focusing the rays of the sun through a magnifying glass. Harnessing the strengths of your employees can start a fire of innovation in your organization.

Authentic Cultures Cultivate the Best Leaders

An organization is only as strong as its leadership. Authentic cultures tend to create leaders from within who rise to higher and higher levels of success. This type of culture improves leadership succession with a steady pool of highly- qualified leaders. These leaders know just how they are wired; they've embraced the power of their own stories and aligned with the organization's Story; they're guided by specific and deeply-ingrained values. This is a big reason why an authentic culture gives an organization such a strong competitive advantage—it can't be replicated, and neither can their leaders.

Authentic Cultures Produce Energized and Engaged Brand Warriors

When most business leaders talk about culture, it's the same-old-same-old: here are our corporate values, here is the HR handbook, and here is our mission statement. But building and sustaining an authentic culture is not about putting words on paper. It's about striking an emotional chord within people's hearts, creating a rallying point they believe in, and understanding that "one hill they'd be willing to die on" for the organization.

The result is brand warriors who have a "take the hill, or else" attitude—from a front-line obsession with customer engagement, to the production facilities, and all the way to the board room. An authentic culture gives you the clarity to discover and focus on that ONE THING that matters most to your organization's success.

Authentic Cultures Become Idea Factories

In the typical workday, how much of an employee's time is spent (aka wasted) worrying about interpersonal issues? Research shows that simply overhearing a negative conversation in the workplace, not even being part of it, decreases productivity significantly. Now multiply that impact by how many times those conversations occur in most organizations and you can see how inauthentic culture can hurt the bottom line. Instead, authentic cultures get intentional about truly connecting people in ways that increase understanding, cohesion, and synergy while minimizing all negative baggage that can come from conflict.

Here's the thing: when people experience negative stress, they go into fight, flight, or freeze mode. Creativity shuts down as their only thought becomes, *How can I get out of here as quickly as possible with some shred of dignity intact?*

On the other hand, when people feel affirmed and mechanisms are in place to provide healthy ways to handle conflict, based on mutual respect for the unique brilliance of everyone involved, the brain is free to do what it does best—create. Instead of being a morgue every Monday, an organization driven by an authentic culture becomes an idea factory where every day feels like Friday.

Authentic Cultures Shift the Focus from Me to We

What drives disruptions on most teams? It is a self-centered, protectionist perspective that causes someone to put his or her interests ahead of others. It's an attitude that says, *As long as my butt gets covered, I'm good.* But in an authentic culture, people are concerned with how best to position themselves to give the greatest value to others. That includes connecting 1-to-1 in an honest way that invites others to do the same.

> An authentic culture becomes an idea factory where every day feels like Friday.

In an authentic culture, the focus begins with *me*—the Big 3—in order to make the most of *we.* Authenticity is never a solo act. It starts with you, but never ends with you. By its very nature, it causes people to realize their own limitations, as well as their strengths, and embrace the need for a team.

Authentic Cultures Fuel Sustainable Growth

The marketplace is full of one-hit wonders—singers, actors, businesses, and brands. Few can pivot to adjust to change. Many struggle to deal with success, a fate that can often prove worse than failure. **Authenticity gives your organization the character within its culture to sustain growth and go beyond its past best performance.** It comes from the heart and soul of the organization's identity—its own unique brilliance.

When the team has the clarity about WHO they are, it fuels their WHY and sustains them by delivering the HOW and the WHAT—regardless of circumstances that may come their way. An organization with an authentic culture thrives over time, because its motivation and inspiration comes from a place deep within, a place circumstances cannot touch.

And there are many more ways authentic cultures empower the best teams to thrive:

Authentic Cultures	Inauthentic Cultures
Passion & Emotion	No Passion & Emotionless
Innovative	Generic
Question status quo	Like-minded followers
Inspiring & motivating	Feels manipulative
Trust Accelerant	Silos & Walls
Focuses on Excellence	Focuses on Competition

Companies with these living, breathing cultures know who they are and live it out—and they eat the competition for breakfast. Just imagine...

➡ An authentic corporate culture so powerful that frontline team members are obsessed with execution excellence.

◯ A company where team members are not only fully engaged on the front lines, they're raving fans of the mission.

◯ A workplace where people are free to maximize strengths and deliver the very best version of themselves to launch performance into the stratosphere.

The result is people obsessed with doing their best because of their love for the organization. Talk about an unprecedented, competitive advantage! Talk about a company employees love!

How Weird Is Your Culture?

So that brings us, not surprisingly, to a simple, but complex question: *How do you know if your culture is weird?*

Through my experiences in the trenches with organizations of all sizes around the globe and across a diverse set of industries, I've come to understand a powerful truth. The Big 3 components that make up who you are as an individual are the same Big 3 components that make up a high-powered, authentic culture: DNA, Story, and Values.

Cultural DNA

The corporate DNA is the individual and collective talents and passion of the people of the organization. Truly authentic cultures create environments that recognize the natural talents and passions of the people. These weird cultures position each person to play to their brilliance advantage, contribute at the highest level, and execute with excellence. The alignments drive team energy levels and sustain them over time.

Companies are wise to pay attention to this DNA early in the hiring and onboarding process, because people determine whether or not the collective DNA of any organization will be toxic. If people are toxic and pessimistic, the organization will have a toxic and pessimistic culture. If they are positive, optimistic, given the opportunity to live out who they are, and contribute in areas of strengths, the organization will have a weird culture—exciting, energetic, and thriving. A company's DNA is its people.

Cultural Story

The corporate Story is just what it sounds like—the organizational history and its defining moments that made it unique and brought it to its current state. Some refer to this as the unique selling proposition, but it's more than that. What survived adversity has given your company its character and uniqueness? La Marzocco survived World War II, floods and Starbucks repositioning. Those defining moments set it up for the weird culture it has today.

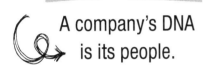

A company's DNA is its people.

On the other hand, what failures or accidents led to your corporate break-throughs? For example, in 1968 Dr. Spencer Silver, a scientist at 3M in the United States, was attempting to develop a super-strong adhesive. He failed, instead creating a low-tack, reusable, pressure-sensitive adhesive by accident. He had no idea what to do with it. For five years, Silver tried selling his "solution without a problem" at 3M but got nowhere. Finally, in 1974 a colleague, Art Fry, who happened to attend one of Silver's seminars tried using the accidental adhesive to hold his hymnal bookmark in place—and the Post-It Note was born. Almost everything about it was accidental, including the choice of yellow paper—their lab only had yellow scrap paper to work with.

Just like you, every culture has these defining moments—successes or failures—that shape its identity. A weird culture identifies those moments and intentionally keeps them alive and central to sustain the passion that produces people with a "frontline obsession" for the mission.

Cultural Values

Corporate values get talked about a lot. Every organization has them written down somewhere, but I think many companies miss the core truth about values. Core values aren't something you desire to have or want to make part of your culture. They are deeply embedded—ingrained from the beginning. They've always been there and will always be there.

Consequently, when I work with organizations to define their core values, I challenge them to be completely honest with themselves and really do some corporate soul-searching to determine if the values they're listing are ones they wish they had, or the ones that are already deeply embedded in the fabric of the company. Those deep values would be the equivalent of your DNA Values.

But in weird organizations, Values don't stop there. Weird companies seek out another set of values, what Patrick Lencioni refers to as *aspirational values*. These are values the organization chooses to aspire to. And you guessed it, those are the cultural Story Values.

For example, a Canadian company I worked with several years ago defined their Core values in this way:

- ⮑ **Integrity:** Committed to doing the right things for the right reasons.
- ⮑ **Passion:** Enthusiasm about what we do to make a difference.
- ⮑ **Tenacity:** We do not give up on our goals or on each other.

As I challenged them to be sure these were the values embedded into the DNA of the organization, they were able to point to numerous examples in the company's history where these values were prevalent.

As I coached them through the discovery process, we discovered that some of the values they were claiming as their core values weren't DNA values at all. They were Story Values, aspirational values they chose to pursue:

- **Accountable:** Own our commitments and expect others to own theirs.

- **Transparency:** Complete, open, and honest communication delivered with respect.

- **Innovation:** Strive to continuously improve people and processes.

The Big 3 guide my work with companies of all sizes, because in reality, every organization is simply a "person," a living, dynamic "organ" that functions in many of the same weird ways.

When we affirm and celebrate each other's weirdness, we create a culture around us that is magical and amazing—and the results make all the work worth it. We give people permission to discover and live out the very best versions of themselves. And when that authenticity goes viral on any team, performance accelerates exponentially.

Chapter 14

The Missing Masterpiece

> "Every block of stone has a statue inside it
> and it is the task of the sculptor to discover it."
> —Michelangelo

Leonardo Da Vinci was one weird dude. The original Renaissance Man, he dabbled in a little bit of everything. His inventions put him ahead of his time. His odd habits made him the talk of his day. But it is his artwork that has made what many consider to be his most significant contribution.

When most people think of DaVinci and painting, they think of the *Mona Lisa* or *The Last Supper*. But it is *Salvator Mundi* that got the world buzzing just a few years ago when it sold for a record-setting price.

Da Vinci painted *Salvator Mundi* later in life, when he was nearly fifty years old, and it is considered to be his finest work, surpassing even the *Mona Lisa* in its artistic genius. It was one of the few paintings Leonardo actually finished, indicating his deep passion for it. It is considered to be the culmination of his illustrious painting journey, a work in which it all came together—his natural talents, his life experiences, and everything he valued in expressing his artistic vision.

But it had been lost to the world.

For centuries after Da Vinci painted it, the painting lived with English royalty, until 1763 when it simply vanished without a trace. No one knows what happened to it until it reappeared in the 19th century, sold as a mere copy of the nearly forgotten Da Vinci masterpiece.

Along the way, the *Salvator Mundi* had layers of paint added to it. No doubt well-intentioned people thought they were "fixing" the masterpiece by applying layers of varnish, or just "touching up" here and there to cover cracks and other perceived blemishes. As a result, the painting's true beauty became concealed.

After another century of being treated as if it were normal, the painting resurfaced at a Sotheby's auction where it was sold to an American for a paltry £45. It remained in the States until 2005 when it was purchased at an estate auction in Louisiana for another trivial amount—and its rediscovery journey began.

One of the new buyers was an Italian Renaissance art guru who thought there just might be something of value beneath the added layers of good intentions. It sure didn't look like much, and it was cracked along the length of the work itself.

Under the care of renowned painting conservator Dianne Dwyer Modestini, the painting's true brilliance slowly began to emerge over the course of a meticulous, five-year restoration process. Upon completion, experts confirmed that the painting was indeed Da Vinci's long-lost masterpiece.

Since then, tens of thousands of people all over the world have stood in line for hours to catch a glimpse of it. Art aficionados have gushed about it. At an auction at Christie's in 2017, the painting sold for a whopping $450 million—the highest tally ever for a single painting!

And to think that for centuries, its brilliance lay hidden beneath layer upon layer of other people's "fixes" and expectations of how it "should" be.

The same may be true for you, my friend. There is no question you are a masterpiece. I hope that is abundantly clear to you after our journey through these pages. You're weird. Your weirdness makes you brilliant and extraordinary. The real you may be hidden beneath years, even decades, of well-intentioned "fixes" and expectation,— the real YOU—have a beauty the world desperately needs to see, and a hole in the universe that needs to be filled by you.

That doesn't mean it will be quick and easy. The process of restoring the Da Vinci masterpiece wasn't either. It took five years to get it right, but it was worth it. On the one hand, it was simple: roll back everything that kept the true real beauty from the world. So it is with you. Discovering the power of you is both simple—your DNA, Story, and Values—yet complex when it comes to revealing that beauty to the rest of the world in a consistently authentic way.

It's not too late to get started. Da Vinci didn't even start his masterpiece until he was nearly fifty years old, in a time when fifty was often considered to be a long life. No matter where you are in your life or career, you can begin to intentionally reveal the masterpiece of YOU to the world. In fact, the Story you've lived to this point is what qualifies you to be *wyrd*, to shape your destiny in a way no one else can. So I don't want to hear any excuses about your being too old or about missed opportunities in life. The best time to be weird is right now.

Many people failed to see the potential of the painting beneath years of good intentions. But that didn't mean it wasn't there. Maybe you've been compromising

> ## The best time to be weird is right now.

yourself for so long you've forgotten what sets your soul on fire. You are comfortable and successful enough but unsatisfied and unfulfilled. Maybe you feel passed over in your career or dismissed as a cheap imitation in life, as if no one has ever really expressed how valuable you truly are. Maybe you feel as if no one has ever believed in you. Like the Da Vinci painting, you feel lost, misplaced, or overlooked.

Good news—you don't have to stay where you are. You can choose to engage the process of discovering and revealing your true brilliance. And now you know you're not alone. I believe in you. Everyone in the *Be Weird* clan believes in you.

The question is: do you believe in the awesomeness of you? I hope so. Are you committed to living out who you are with authenticity in a way that invites others to do the same thing? If so, greatness lies ahead.

Don't miss this. What makes the painting so valuable? It's not the unprecedented price it got at auction. Don't get me wrong, $450 million is a lot of money, but that's still a value assigned to it by someone else. As anyone who appreciates fine art will tell you, the Salvator Mundi is not worth $450 million. As conservator put it, the Salvator Mundi is "one of the most important expressions that Leonardo left us... so the price doesn't matter." It's priceless. One-of-a kind. Irreplaceable. A true masterpiece.

In the years left to you on this planet, you have the *only* opportunity to steward the brilliance of YOU. One day, someone somewhere will talk about your legacy. What they say will depend on how well you do *you*, because if you don't do you, YOU won't get done. And that would be a tragedy, because there is no one else like you. Deep down, you can feel it. When you read these words, you feel the truth of them in your soul.

I know the tension within. As a young professional, I believed like many people do that I would have to choose one of two paths—fit in, be normal, and achieve what other people defined as success or blaze my own trail and embrace my weirdness. I thought I had to choose between success and fulfillment. In the face of that supposed conundrum, I chose to follow my own authentic way. I chose to follow my heart and listen to the weird voice inside. Even if it meant I would never achieve success as defined by everyone else, I refused to swim in a sea of sameness.

I can't say the journey has always been easy. In fact, sometimes this road has been full of hardships, heartaches and frustration. But it is my Story—it is ME—lived out in my own weird way. As a result it has been an exhilarating, purposeful, and deeply fulfilling journey.

I invite you to take the challenge with me—choose to *be weird.*

Yes, it will be *not* normal. Yes, it will be weird. But I promise you this. When you do celebrate your weirdness—and the weirdness of everyone around you—you'll feel your soul rise up again as you leave normal behind and finally start where your Story began—with *who* you are and how you can *maximize the power* of you in every area of life.

What I've discovered is this: choosing to be weird means you don't have to choose between success or fulfillment. Being weird is the embodiment of both. Both voices are clamoring for your attention—the voice of conformity and sameness or the weird voice within that calls you to Be You with unrelenting passion!

Which voice will you listen to?

Don't be afraid of being weird. Be afraid of being like everyone else. It's OK to live a life others don't understand.

If you don't do you, YOU won't get done.

Visit *BeWeird.com* to join the Be Weird clan.
Get inspiration and insights and—above all—connect with other people like you who are committed to succeeding in business and life by being authentic.

Acknowledgments

Although this book reflects what I've learned over the last thirty years in business and fifty-eight years of life, it couldn't have been written without the support of friends, associates and clients. Foremost among them is Bill Blankschaen. Your weirdness and talent were the perfect fit for me. Your patience and contribution was paramount in the completion of this book. Many times, you were able to take my ideas and express them better than me.

I also owe a debt of gratitude to so many of my business clients who continuously encouraged me to share my weirdness through this book. Without your encouragement, I would have never started the process much less completed it.

I want to thank the people whose stories are presented here. Thank you Sam Riley, who may be the weirdest man I know. Thanks to Al Bennett who has been as much a friend as a business associate and is most comfortable in his own skin. I owe a tremendous debt of gratitude to Kelly, Lindsey, and Roseanne at Kindercare. Your dedication and love towards children and nurturing who they are naturally is an inspiration to me. I have cherished our work together. And finally, I want to thank the weird folks at La Marzocco, especially Chris and Guido. You have shown me the power of a weird culture. I cherish the relationship we have.

I would also like to acknowledge some very special people in my life. Chris Goede, who took a chance and gave me an opportunity when I needed it most. Little did I know that would be the beginning of a journey that would provide many of the stories reflected in this book.

Without question I must recognize my friend and business colleague Jason Grant. "Grantino," without you trusting me, many of the business relationships in this book wouldn't be in here. I am thankful for the business we've conducted together over the years.

Michael Bryant, you have been a quiet but solid rock in my life. Your patience in listening to my rambling and your quiet wisdom have contributed much to my story. You are a coach to a coach and I value you more than you'll ever know.

I must also acknowledge my friend Corey Baker. Where would I be without those 2:00 am talks? Your friendship helped me through one of the toughest times of my life.

All of you expand my horizons and are a constant source of inspiration and strength.

Endnotes

Chapter 1
[1] Bilmes, Alex. "Jay-Z on his music, politics, and his violent past." *GQ*. 2005.
http://www.gq-magazine.co.uk/article/jay-z-interview-music-politics-violence

Chapter 4
[2] https://www.complex.com/sports/2017/03/the-oral-history-of-michael-jordan-baseball-career
[3] Ira Berkow "A Humbled Jordan Learns New Truths." *The New York Times*. 1994.
https://www.nytimes.com/1994/04/11/sports/a-humbled-jordan-learns-new-truths.html
[4] "Lou Gehrig Quotes". *Baseball-Almanac.com*. Archived from the original on 2 April 2007.
Retrieved 2007-04-25.
[5] http://www.businessinsider.com/steve-jobs-former-publicist-andy-cunningham-reality-distor
tion-field-apple-2017-11
[6] O'Neill, Thomas P.. "Frenemies: A Love Story." *The New York Times*. October 5, 2012.
https://campaignstops.blogs.nytimes.com/2012/10/05/frenemies-a-love-story/
[7] Riley, Sam. Interview by Bill Blankschaen. Personal interview. Atlanta, August 26, 2017.
[8] Riley, Sam. Interview by Bill Blankschaen. Personal interview. Atlanta, August 26, 2017.

Chapter 5
[9] Stephen Pressfield, *Turning Pro: Tap your Inner Power and Create Your Life's Work*.
New York, NY: Black Irish Entertainment LLC, 2012.
[10] James Carville, Paul Begala. *Buck Up, Suck Up ... and Come Back When You Foul Up:
12 Winning Secrets from the War Room*. New York, NY: Simon & Schuster, 2002.
[11] The Pixar story I reference at various times in the book is drawn primarily from *The Pixar
Touch: The Making of a Company*, by David A. Price, Vintage Books, 2008.

Chapter 6
[12] Rory Vaden, *Procrastinate on Purpose: 5 Permissions to Multiply Your Time*. P. 196.

Chapter 7
[13] Hillenbrand, Laura. *Unbroken*. New York, NY: Random House LLC, 2010.;
https://news.usc.edu/1836/the-great-zamperini/
[14] Larsen, Gail. *Transformational Speaking: If You Want to Change the World, Tell a Better
Story*. Berkley, CA: Celestial Arts, 2007. P. 15.

Chapter 8

[15] Speigel, Alex, host. "The New Normal." *Invisibilia.* NPR, June 17, 2016. https://www.npr.org/2016/06/17/482443233/listen-to-the-episode.

[16] http://www.businessinsider.com/lebron-james-body-care-workouts-diet-insane-2017-10.

[17] Thompson, Wright, "How Tiger Woods' Life Unraveled in the years after father Earl Woods death." *ESPN.* April 21, 2016. http://www.espn.com/espn/feature/story/_/id/15278522/how-tiger-woods-life-unraveled-years-father-earl-woods-death.

[18] Ziglar, Zig. *See You at the Top.* Gretna, LA: Pelican Publishing Company, 2000.

Chapter 9

[19] Pile, Stephen. *The Book of Heroic Failures.* 1979.

[20] *Darkest Hour.* Dir. Joe Wright. Perf. Gary Oldman, Lily James, Ben Mendelsohn, and Kristin Scott Thomas. Focus Features. 2017.

[21] Levesque, Ryan. *Ask.* Dunham Books: 2015.

Chapter 10

[22] *National Treasure.* Dir. Jon Turteltaub. Perf. Nicolas Cage, Diane Kruger, and Justin Bartha. Walt Disney Pictures and Jerry Bruckheimer Films, 2004. DVD.

[23] Godin, Seth. "In Praise of the Purple Cow." *Fast Company,* January 31, 2003. https://www.fastcompany.com/46049/praise-purple-cow.

[24] McKeown, Greg. *Essentialism: The Disciplined Pursuit of Less.* New York, NY: Random House LLC, 2014. P. 10.

Chapter 11

[25] Bennett, Al. Interview by Bill Blankschaen. Personal Interview. May 24, 2018.

[26] Tugaleva, Vironika. *The Love Mindset.*

[27] Price, David A.. *The Pixar Touch: The Making of a Company.* Vintage Books, 2008.

Chapter 12

[28] Oborn, Glennie, and Kelley Oborn. Interviews by Bill Blankschaen. Personal interviews. November 25-27, 2017.

[29] Adkins, Amy. "Employee Engagement in U.S. Stagnant in 2015." http://news.gallup.com/poll/188144/employee-engagement-stagnant-2015.aspx

[30] Eisenhauer, Tim. "20 Fundamental Problems Linked to Employee Disengagement." https://axerosolutions.com/blogs/timeisenhauer/pulse/365/20-fundamental-problems-linked-to-employee-disengagement.

[31] Cloud, Henry. *Boundaries for Leaders.* New York, NY: HarperCollins Publishers, 2013.

[32] Peters, Tom. *the Pursuit of WOW.* New York, NY: Random House LLC, 2010.